Search For
A Whisky Bothy

Search For
A Whisky Bothy

Ralfy

Published by Irish Sea Trading Co. Ltd:,
Ramsey,
Isle Of Man,
IM7 1HG

SEARCH FOR A WHISKY BOTHY
Second Edition

Warning – If you choose to drink alcohol and are of legal age to do
so in your Country of residence, drink in moderation, with
consideration, and know your healthy limits for the sake of yourself
and those around you.

Condition of sale

ISBN 978-1-916-25750-4

Book formatted by www.bookformatting.co.uk.

Contents

This book is dedicated to malt-mates.

With regards !

Prologue

It was shortly after a passing, and casually delivered comment on my online YouTube Channel 'ralfydotcom' where I routinely present spirit review vlogs that I mentioned, "perhaps I should write a book to celebrate ten years of ralfydotcom". The response was immediate and heart-warming with many subscribers showing interest in buying my book, ... if I actually wrote it.

After two false starts in 2018, and after too much reference to other written books, I finally got my own theme and content into my mind in the correct order, and the rest, well. . . you will find in this book.

I would like to thank everyone I have met through the years for contributing their whisky-related input into a life less-ordinary, and one which by accident has been fueled by regular small portions of good quality liquor.

Special shout out to my guest editors and feed-backers, John, Jo, Andy, Pete, Roddy and Paul who first-scanned the chapters I sent to them in order that I avoid serious self-delusions and get it right.

Thanks to Lulu.com who, due to the internet, have provided a good quality, self-publishing platform for writers who may be of no particular interest to traditional publishers.

A big malty-mention to Partick in Glasgow, Glasgow's Whisky Club, The Bon Accord pub people in North Street, Charing Cross, and all the decent folks I have met over the years connected to the Scotch Whisky Industry. It's never ever been a waste of time, I have enjoyed every minute and intend to enjoy a few more over the next few years.

Slante!

youtube.com, channel - 'ralfydotcom'

Chapter One

First Impressions Always Remain

Over Time

Notes.

A young and spirit-driven malt moment suggestive of yester-year tinged with nostalgia, drama and complex booze-cabinet notes of rum, single malt, Benedictine, another li-queur and cheap blended scotch. Simple form but memora-ble notes of sweetness and sour-complex with a residual bit-ter soft glow.

I was only four years old but already spreading my little wings of independence in getting to know the world around me which seemed so big and endless possessing infinite complexities which in turn registered regularly, but briefly in my small head now and again. I sensed the thrill of big adventures and the awareness that these adventures began with faltering steps in the right direction.

One of the first steps to present itself was observing the expres-sion of true contentment on my father's face as he sat during winter nights in front of a gas fireplace, listening to renaissance music playing on his record player, whilst carefully sipping malt whisky from a little thimble glass. It was a moving sight to an impression-able boy about to start school and looking for inspiration and ambi-tion... it sort of worked.

I asked for a smell, he held down the glass and let me experi-ence the first sour nip of ethanol accompanied by grain and honey then, summoning up courage I asked for a sip, just a tiny sip, and he chuckled to himself as parental responsibility subsided in favour of the potential entertainment value.

It was a shock, a blast of bitter, sour, horrible, nasty 'flames' which had nothing of the cloying sweetness I was familiar with in my sweets, cereals and puddings. I spat out the residue onto the woolly sleeve of my jumper and headed through to the kitchen for sugar, with the laughter of my dad following me along the hallway. Even as a spoon of white crystals kindly provided by my sympathetic mum sprinkled it's way over the tongue, I briefly experienced an intense dizzy jab of alcohol intoxication, fleeting, powerful and exciting in its unfamiliarity. Father appeared at the kitchen door, "Kettle on", he said, then laughed, "Guess I keep the Rosebank to myself then, this chap wont be raiding the cupboard for a while". Mum glanced back towards the heating kettle smiling to herself.

The Rosebank had been as a gift from a grateful client, a lover of books, a rare quality in that too few of us really understand how important to the calibre of humanoid survival the informations found in books actually are.

He started as a humble librarian at Hutchesontown Public Library in Glasgow looking after restless bored young children who would have read, if only they could have read, along with elderly housewives, searching methodically for more pulp romance to try to improve the hum-drum routine of their boring lives, shackled through marriage vows and religious intimidation to tired, overworked, dull, and often aggressive husbands.

Slowly, over time he progressed to higher office, graduating to departmental head of the History and Topography Department at the Mitchell Reference Library, Charing Cross, Glasgow, europe's largest public reference and book research Institution.

It still is a grand and imposing stone edifice toped with a large green copper dome to express it's credentials as a worthy hub of knowledge. My dad loved his job.

Part of that love was to advise on the restoration of books, and engagement of professional restorers of old books and manuscripts, a rare set of skills possessed by too few people who were only to be found when contacted through the right contacts, including my dad.

Occasionally he would be approached for advice and direction by book-lovers and after supplying encouragement and contacts would receive as civil consideration a bottle of whisky which he preferred to anything else. This was the reason that on regular occasions another obscure bottle of something precious would suddenly appear in the drinks cabinet. Macallan, Talisker, Rosebank, Highland Park, Laphroaig... all different . . . rarely the same, some had ages stated on them whilst some did not, and even now it was the 'presence' of the Rosebank that I remember the most. A standard but charismatic bottle of dark olive green with white cap foil and label stating "Rosebank, celebrated pure malt SCOTCH WHISKY 70 Proof made in Falkirk".

On the label was a crest in red, black and white showing a little bird in a sort of nest surrounded by barley stalks. I just don't know why, but at such a young age I connected to the bottle in a way I could simply not understand. It was the just start of a special relationship, a grail quest, an unfathomable adventure, something wonderful.

Starting school for the first time was only a few weeks away, and as nothing was planned and holidays nearly over, I was bored and restless in a subdued and silent house where the walls began to feel a little prison-like.

The drinks cabinet called out to me, but as it was in the do-not-enter room for gas fires and guests only, I could not go in alone. The drinks cabinet called out to me again, softy, more dangerously, enticingly me, I was only four, I was only a boy and I relented to the magnetism of that cabinet and its bottles. I sneaked towards the room pausing to listen intently for a response from my mother in the kitchen, preparing the evening dinner, but thanks to the crackle of the BBC broadcasting through the transistor radio, she seemed oblivious to my mischief.

The door was locked, there was not a key, this was to be my first challenge.

I wandered through to the kitchen and looked inquisitively at my mother, she ignored me and remained busy in the meal preparation, boiled stew, parsnips and new potatoes. I moved back to the hall-way and stared again at the locked door, almost imagining it to open suddenly as I thought the words 'open sesame', but the door remained defiantly closed. Orlando the family ginger tom cat ambled by thinking of food, as he always had his most neutral expression when his appetite re-rumbled his tummy. He glanced briefly towards me in unaffected sympathy and moved towards the stair cupboard, a discreet triangular space beside the bathroom. He stopped, rubbed the door with his face and scuttled off before I could give him a lift-up and a hug. Only a latch secured the stair cupboard door, but on bending down and entering the dusty, musty dim-lit, closed space I found the key on a string attached to a hook, just out of reach but not too far... now suddenly remembered from long ago.

I now posessed the key which would access the door and enable the adventure. Behind the now unlocked door was silence, late-summer light and a cosyness one gets with simple, but comfortable rooms. Nothing fancy, a thin carpet overthrown with a quality persian rug and finished with three chairs which was enough as visitors were rare, also, a vinyl turntable record player, a gas fire, and a discreet victorian dark wood drinks cabinet, resplendent with mirrors, ornate ivory inlay and history.

I slowly closed the door behind me, all the while listening for kitchen sounds of a mother on the warpath, but there was nothing, just silence and calm.

The cupboard was three times my height, austere and weathered by auction house storage, the top being decorated with finials and tiny wooden railings, all inlayed and showing fine craftsmanship. My glance moved down past the protruding shelf which held the 'nibbles', assorted nuts, turkish delight, jelly figs and chocolate in cut-glass plates which added finesse to holidays, birthdays and New Year celebrations. I finally arrived at my head-height with a small ornamental key already in the brass lock which secured the alcohol cupboard shut.

Two twists, and the door was opened revealing bottles of gems, mysteries and magic, along with an ambient smell of old polish, vintage book paper and subtle spirity grain, fruit, sugar, spice and fire-smoke smells.

There were five bottles in residence, and all were opened with varying levels of fill, two plain small paris wine goblets, a thimble sized cut-glass ornamental drinking glass and an old chipped water jug from a bar were all placed neatly inside. The five bottles met my gaze as if reunited with their old friend, deep inside of me turbulent invisible subconscious waves broke through the still waters of my conscious world suggesting previous incarnations of a life in love with liquor, this soporific balm and elixir which can shield us so well from the real world around us. I felt my heart race as young hands reached out to embrace old friends made of glass, cork and paper.

I lifted out the first bottle, solid, very heavy, nearly full and with a brick-red label featuring a battle ship on a choppy sea, "Top Dog" the label said.

I was sure that the ship was the S.S. Top Dog because that would be a really great name for a battle ship. "Fine Old Demerara rum" it continued as way of introduction, I stumbled to understand the word 'demerara' so I just called it 'hurra' instead and imagined all the jolly sailors aboard the 'Top Dog' tucking into flagons of Top Dog Grog courtesy of an eternally grateful Captain who understood the best way to keep the ship content was coal in the boiler, potatoes on the plates and watered-rum in the ship-mates bellies!

I unscrewed the white foil top and put my nose to the neck of the bottle. Toffee, muscovado, vanilla, sweets and tobacco assaulted my nose. The clear glass revealed a dark mahogany liquor which filled my nose with images of sunsets, crashing waves and dusky maidens singing songs on sea shores with no cares to the World. The bottle was tipped slowly and carefully towards the white metal cap now in my other hand and with a soft glugging sound a small splash of the amber liquid settled into the cap, I drank it, coughed and suddenly spat out the remainder of what I was expecting to swallow, it was overpoweringly bitter, sour, dark-flavoured and most of all, nippy, like a thousand piranhas were suddenly feeding on my tongue. Rum splashed off the bottle's label as I returned the unwanted remains and tightened back the screw top. Trembling at my crime I deposited it back to it's original position next to the Rosebank.

From Caribbean islands to Northern Europes' shores, one bottle to the next bottle and sitting so close to one another but of such different provenance and history, from cane to grain, from hot sun to grey clouds, a very different experience indeed. After a few minutes of trying to unscrew the cork on the whisky bottle I eventually noticed that instead of it spinning and squeaking inside the neck, I had to pull, and pull again to get the cork to shift. It pulled out suddenly, loudly with a loud 'plop' and I froze, expecting my mother to suddenly loom over me with crossed arms and a stern "I'm going to have to tell your father", but it never happened, nothing, the spell was intact, as silently as I could I reached for the little cut-glass thimbler and poured my first wee illicit dram which was far easier to do than with the bottle of rum, as the contents were laying low as if declaring the preference over several weeks for grain over cane by my father.

It was just a little drop but the smell was euphoric; sunny summer days, golden barley fields and gentle autumn skies, I felt the presence in the nose of yesterday's halcyon and precious quiet moments full of positivity, contentment and barley-suger sweets that I enjoyed so much, sold at the local newsagents shop every Wednesday, and where I was allowed to buy whilst returning home from somewhere.

It was sublime as the smell grew and crescendoed, filling the cupboard with a lust for life that is only found in happy fields of golden, living sun-bearing ripe seeds full of the days presence and nourishment. I could sense the yeast, the barrel oak wood, the grain, fruits, vanilla and exotic spices only previously encountered in the local grocer's shop, and biscuits, beautiful, creamy rich tea biscuits. The smell was good, so good... *and* with biscuits too.

I sipped the liquor, the swift, abrupt explosion hit like a roaring tidal break on a rolling frothy wave of burning alcohol, nipping, nipping, nipping more, I coughed, spat and pulled my sleeve quickly across my numbing lips, too much, too harsh, too soon; - I realised that adventures needed discomfort and bad-bits but this was more than enough for now, I tipped the remaining whisky back into the bottle and replaced the cork, as if putting a sprytly genie back into a lamp.

With numb lips and trembling hands I left the silence of the room and made my way through to the kitchen and in a slightly over-intense way and asked "Can I have a glass of milk mum . . . please?"

"Of course dear! . . . there you go", she added, passing a cold mug of full-fat milk towards my grateful, outstretched hands. I drank quickly and returned to the scene of my crime surprised that my mothers usual instincts had not rumbled me by now.

The next bottle for examination was more squat, green and with what looked like a plumber's weld of lead around the folded shiny seal.

Again, a cork, which thanks to previous experience, I removed with ease.

This bottle was not opened as often as the others, as my father preferred less sugary concoctions, and small deposits of sugar crystals crackled and crunched as I removed the stopper and poured a little of the greenish thick syrup into the still wet but empty thimble glass. D.O.M. is what the small circular label read, which I did not understand so concluded that it was made from DOM juice. There were signs that a smaller label had been in place at the base of the bottle, but it had fallen off at some point, and as such, I ignored the omission although I knew there would be a reason, but it did not matter as the content would surely be very tasty due to the red wax seal stamped onto the side of the bottle, it was very imposing and I was very impressed.

This was different from the others, like a gardener's walled garden protected from wind, frosts and elemental violence of all the four seasons, and full of precious fragrant herbs and perennials pulling butterflies and bees from miles around to feast on the nectar of mother nature's variety. Sage, thyme, coriander, mint, lovage, fennel, honey dew, and basil, confusing, medicinal and gloriously sweet. I let the medication slip slowly across my tongue, and onwards coating my little throat like the intense mixture I had been given the last time I had caught a cold and was laying in bed feeling oh-so sorry for myself, and wishing my little brother Clive was as badly off as I was, but he wasn't, which made my suffering all the worse. I had enjoyed the cough mixture medicine a lot, but this was better, much, much better and far more impacting in it's reassurance and warmth.

I poured a small second glass, tracing the glow of alpine meadows, resinous tree barks and confused herbs, and it was exquisite, but it was not as good as the first taste This time I felt an unexpected brief moment of dizziness, nausea, imbalance and confusion, but it passed as quickly as it arrived!

I gingerly slid the bottle back into its place within the cupboard making sure the label was facing the front, just as I found it, and then turned my attention to the last bottle.

Tall and shapely, brown glass with a black plastic screw top, and dominated by an imposing English mustard yellow label displaying an oriental doorway into a sun-blasted scene of swaying palm trees and fluffy clouds. I could not read the odd-looking name on the label but underneath it was the statement 'product of Mexico'.

This was to me the most ethereal of all the bottles, it just seemed to be so special with the reference to an exotic location somewhere else in the World far-flung and very, very different.

The liquor awaited, and the small glass was refilled with a much darker mahogany-coloured viscous juice.

I was fascinated as the first sip passed my lips bringing welcoming sweetness, deep spicy and aromatic notes of equatorial promise, infused with unknown and unrecognisable stuff, lots and lots of very yummy stuff.

I poured another glass, holding the sweetness and flavours on my tongue for as long as I could, it was nectar.

Whilst consumed by this magic a strange and subtle wave of disorientation whispered at the back of my head, but then departed as swiftly as it had arrived. Two minutes later as I finished a third glass of the dark brown fondant, then more quickly than realised, the surge of dizziness returned with reinforcements this time, and hurried across my head spinning the cupboard and room constantly in one direction... then my personal alarm bells started clanging, this, was just not right.

The bottles were checked, the cupboard was closed and even as I started to leave the room the door went wobbly and my knees gave way under me as a storm-sized version of the previous small surge in disorientation arrived, suddenly, shockingly, totally.

I hit the carpet by the door and lay terrified by this sudden frightening event, this time the feeling remained and did not subside, it was growing worse.

Panicked, I hurridly reached for the front door and out of the house, exiting around the peripheral garden path retreating in wavy lines to the rear of the house to where my father's motorcycle shed was. It was locked, but the space behind it was accessible between the wood hut and the privet hedge, an area, small and discreet that I used as a den. Orlando the cat had got there first and seemed genuinely upset as I dropped to my knees, braced myself with my hands, looked into mother-earth for gravity, support and assurances, then I threw up into the hedge, briefly startling a perching blackbird which flew away chirping loudly and tutting at me as it went. Orlando trotted off to the house, I backed away from the pool of still-warm sick and with a deep breath, buried my head onto a pile of dead leaves and swiftly fell asleep.

When I awoke later all was silent and sunny with the shadows of the day stretching slowly away from the descending sun turning from iridescent yellow globe to mellowed blurry orange sphere as it sank over the trees lined up across the road. I groaned, my head was sore, my nose was squashed , my ankle which had become caught up in the hedge was stiff and numb, the birds sang in the trees, and Orlando the cat sauntered back as if to check on proceedings, he almost seemed concerned.

It was two weeks later that my father informed my brother and I that although we were young we had a grown-up job to do in keeping an eye on our mother who, we were told, 'needed support with a problem!'.

My brother and I were, of course, confused, why would we need to spend time watching our mum's problem, she seemed to do that fine by herself without assistance.

On returning from work my father had noticed the room door improperly closed, the liquor cupboard unlocked, and a small, empty wet glass inside smelling strongly of coffee. For several months my mother was civilly requested to drink tea, and as she did as she was told, the problem seemed to sort itself out!

Over fifty years later I am sitting on a hillside above the local town on an island that I now call home. A seat is unfolded, a three-legged side-table is anchored down with polythene bags filled with foraged stones and now supporting a glass, a water jug and bottle, I am ready to commence Ralfy Review 600 called 'Rosebank on a windy day'.

I don't drink many versions of Rosebank these days as they are too expensive, and there are too few good versions worth bothering about, but I have one, a good, bitter, dry and astringent-grainy one and I am enjoying it a lot. As one of the great 'Rare Malt Selection' range it is very competent and ultimately rewarding in both smell and taste.

Suddenly a flurry of wind whips round from behind a copse of trees, huddled at the top of the local reservoir, my glass tips over, scattering the contents across the table surface, I react quickly by restabilizing the glass and carefully pouring the spilt malt back into the compact vessel. Some is inevitably lost into the earth below but much is saved due to the wooden trim round the rim of the table top and I feel quite pleased about my instantaneous responsive reaction to the crisis.

I continue to record the vlog which goes very well, if slightly chilly, despite some glancing rays of sunshine and a little seasonal warmth in the air. With a handy remote control button I click off the recording camera and listen in silence to the landscape around me, it is beautiful, I sip from the glass in my hand, the calibre of event does not pass me by and I see the connection of sight, sound, smell and taste in perfect accord, harmonious with the growing wave of nostalgia that rolls across my mind animating, amplifying and reminding me in detail of my first illicit encounter with this charismatic malt.

It's strange how memory plays tricks on us, with a near-lost far-distant memory of things we think happened, but *sort of* happened in a different way. The recollection can suddenly be intense if the situation is 'right' and I laugh to myself at the thought of my four year old self grandly sipping single malt with appreciation when this in fact was most certainly not the case.

The moment then was far more laced with sugar syrup, awareness of wrong-doing, and retrospective alertness to that moment in my life being one where I never actually got caught and subsequently made accountable for my wrong-doing. The joys of successful crime are special to a child, less so to an adult, and the difference is made up for with nostalgia.

I raise my glass, sip, savour, stop and head back to my van for coffee and cake. Good stuff!

The upload can happen tomorrow, vlog out on Sunday, comments reviewed on Monday.

Chapter Two

Discovering Malt-Moments

And Malt-Mates

Notes

Malty arrival, full-bodied turning fruity, cereal, vanilla, and notes of city and toffee. A comfortable experience, undemanding and for the fire-side at home on a winter's night. Complex and memorable finish with hints of old casks from yester-year.

The front door knocked, I answered it, the stranger was a tired but civil-looking, youngish and thin man with short dark hair and wearing a functional, budget-selected business suit with a mismatching squinty tie, and who on my appearance promptly lifted out a sealed bottle of whisky from his tatty brown leather case, and offered it to me with a slow and affirming grin.

This was both unexpected and a bit odd. Nothing in the way of introduction, no 'hello', no 'would you like to buy this bottle?'

I stood, consciously folding my arms so as to form a convincing barrier to the possible 'hard sell' technique I thought I was being subjected to.

He grinned, "Sorry", he said "I was just being cheeky, it's been a long day and my feet are killing me now, would you like a bottle of whisky?"

I paused, arms still crossed. He read my body-language and shifted course in his pitch.

"It's free, part of our feed-back marketing to see how people in Glasgow like the new Bell's Islander, it's traditional Bells with a wee peaty twist for extra", he added "It's marketing so there's no charge, all we ask is for feed-back and comments".

"Okay", I responded, "So there's not a charge and the bottle's free for me to drink!"

"Yes", he replied, he smiled, and concluded, "Could you just drop-off a few notes on it down at the Smithy Pub on the main road", he pointed in the general direction of one of the local bars, "That would be really helpful... oh, and thanks", he shouted, waving a hand above his head as he trotted off back down the worn stairs of my traditional Glasgow close and out the front door onto Gardner Street, Partick.

I stood at the front door of my flat, bought only the month previously, and just beginning to feel homely and 'mine', and looked down at the bottle in my hand.

Bells

Islander

Mature Scotch Whisky

Island & Islay Malts

Under the 'Islander' bit there was a small rustic picture of a white cottage and surrounding buildings somewhere highland, and with a wee boat. The label looked boring.

I twisted off the screw top which popped loose with a light metallic crack, and still standing at my front door took a swig straight out the bottle. It was harsh, nippy, peaty, malty, grainy, cereally.. . rough!

At this moment the letterbox opposite my door fluttered briefly and less than three seconds later the familiar rattle of a security chain being un-coupled sounded, and my new neighbour across the landing threw open his door, staring accusingly at me across the close.

"Bit early for that, is it not?" he glared, then promptly slammed his door leaving the letterbox chattering in alarm for a second, before scuttling down the stairs.

I just smiled sweetly but *firmly* as he passed, saying nothing, and then retreated behind my own front door closing it with a thud.

I'm sure he got the message the judgemental teetotal wee bastard.

He could get stuffed!

I pulled a glass tumbler from off of the kitchen draining board, and some ice was pulled out of the freezer compartment of my fridge. Splash, splash, plop, plop, glass, whisky, ice.

I decided at this point, whilst it was cooling, to light my coal fire in the front room. Fifteen minutes after the match had spluttered out from completing it's task, the fire roared into life and into flames.

My glass and I settled down to an evening of silence, dancing embers glowing in the hearth and into my soft intoxication. Over the next few hours the whisky seemed to mellow and sweeten reminding me of my first contact, or should I say my first 'conversation' with whiskies all these years ago in my fathers liquor cabinet. I was in no hurry to get drunk, it was no race to me, no mad dash, as it seems to be for so many around us in this madding world.

For me it was an amble, a stroll, a wander through time, companion flames from a warm hearth and the blissful wall of silence, cosiness and companionship of my own room.

That was just the way it was for me back in the 1980s, and over the decades very little has changed.

Even now I most enjoy whisky in silence, alone, and in the presence of sunshine or fire, or both together are even better. Company is good, but the best company is on my own and with a dram.

I have made it a habit in life to stick to promises, as I have an instinctive awareness that personal integrity is an undervalued form of wealth, enhancing the quality and meaning of our lives, and from experience over many years I find this to be generally true. Early in life there were a few exceptions as a result of circumstances and confusion, however as a life-guide rule it tends to work very well and provide unexpected rewards, often influenced by 'chance', that morphing, and universal certainty. A week later as the sun set on another cluttered and forgotten day, I made my way down to the local bar as requested by the whisky-giver, and having carefully selected a quiet time of the evening, I went to fulfil my obligation.

With half of a bottle of Bells Islander and a packet of digestive biscuits in my hands I entered through a wide, and ornamental frosted glass door, into a spacious public area decorated with mixed coloured wooden walls, and hard-wearing functional furniture evenly spaced across a dark planked and foot-worn floor.

To further decorate this space, liquor advertising mirrors adorned the walls, spaced out so as not to require too many, and patinated by dust, tobacco smoke and time. Yellowed ceiling lights mocking the style of a chandelier, and in attempted grandeur, cast yellowish light downwards setting a pleasant but subdued atmosphere conducive to prolonged recreational drinking. The smell of pine and beer-stale urine wafted ethereally from out of an opened toilet door at the back of the bar and to complete the functionality of the space, on the right hand side stood a modest long-benched dark-wood bar with intermittent extra lighting, to enhance the presence of assorted liquor bottles on shelves along with assorted bags of nuts, crisps and packets of hand-rolling tobacco.

Beer pumps adorned with fresh drying clothes were spaced irregularly, like broken lower teeth, along the bar top, and in the middle of this stood a fading, patient greyish man looking the wrong size of too thin and puffing rather slowly and methodically on a wilting cigarette.

"Can I get you anything pal", he asked languidly, unhurried by years of experience in his job and in life. "Er, the whisky chap in a suit came to my door and gave me this", I flourished the dying bottle of Islander.

He smiled knowingly, "Ay, fine then, do I get to finish the rest of that?" he chuckled.

"He said to come here and give you my opinion", I glanced again to the bottle, "I've written down some stuff on it if I can leave it with you for him".

The bar man leaned across between two shining pumps and commented "Actually you're the only one who's bothered so far, I was expecting others, but that's Glasgow for you, indifference in the face of generosity". He seemed civil and curious so I sat down on the nearest bar stool and parked the bottle next to me.

"I suppose I should buy a pint", I said, half thinking aloud.

"Good start to the night", he responded, "What's it tae be ?"

I glanced at the badges on the handles, "pint of Youngers No3 please".

"No3 coming up pal, good choice, it's fresh on", he glanced over, "And better then 'ur lager", he winked, appreciating my civility and thoughtfulness in selection.

I sipped the beer, it was cool, malty, aromatic, I promptly sipped again, this time a little more volume and a little bit faster.

It was just at this moment that I became aware of another person in the bar, a noise of scuffing shoe soles drawing my glance across the place to the opened door of the gents toilet where a small, squat older man appeared, slightly unsteady, and with an abnormally red face hiding behind thick tortoise shell plastic brown glasses. His long dirty silver hair tied back in a pony tail and a green, sleeveless padded jacket with rather large pockets hovered above a slightly stained pair of soft baggy sports pants clearly in need of a washing machine.

He shuffled to the bar with the stale but aromatic smell of whisky proceeding him by a few yards.

"'Nuther one James, and fur ficks sake no ice", he muttered, looking at his handful of coins some of which started to fall on the floor. The barman pulled a small fresh tumbler from the draining rack above the sink and wedged it under an optic. A 1/3gill was delivered, glugging from out of a large upturned magnum bottle of Bells hanging securely off the shelf.

The fallen coins were left where they fell, a testament to a life less alert.

James the barman paused in releasing hold of the glass as he slid it across the counter, "That will be your last today Sanny, no more... not today".

Wee Sanny tutted, casting his bleary eyes to the ornate ceiling, looking offended, but saying nothing. Turning to me standing next to him, and as if for assurance and support, he addressed me.

"Just a terrible, terrible shame son", he pointed to James, "I've watched that boy grow up", he hissed, as if this in itself was enough to reprimand James for his impertinence.

At this point I felt obliged to offer a conversation in an attempt to lighten the growing mood, however I was cut short by Sanny swilling his glass and downing the entire contents in one swig.

I was shocked, he could not have tasted a drop... did he even notice what he was drinking!.

It was still around half six in the evening as Sanny struggled to the door, and swinging it open allowed the street air of car smoke, and rumble of busy humanity, to ease the mood back to normal inside the premises.

James nodded to himself, "Don't let that pint evaporate", he grinned with a wink, glad that a small developing drama in his bar had quickly resolved itself.

I continued to sip slowly from my pint and rummaging in my trouser pocket pulled out a rather crumpled folded sheet of paper. "I wrote down some notes on the 'Islander' if the Whisky guy is interested".

"Some detail here", James declared, "as I just said, most folk haven't bothered to show up yet. In fact you are actually the only one so far", he paused briefly, "I will pass this onto the Rep when he comes in, although he's that busy rushing around the City, so I don't expect to see him for a week at least! I suppose as a good outlet of his, we can be relied upon to forward all the feedback, I think about twelve homes round here got bottles, they don't normally do such extravagance, must be the new manager at the office".

I finished my beer, shook James's hand and left to sort out my dinner.

I took the remains of the 'Islander' with me. Just in case . . .

I had enjoyed the Youngers No3, it was delicious, so it was less than a week later that I wandered back into the Smiddy Bar on Dumbarton road for another pint. James was not behind the bar, but Sanny was on a stool in front of it looking more sober than the last time I saw him.

"How ye' doin' son?" he slurred, "Back to buy me that drink you owe me, eh, eh,?"

I smiled, and pretended to be meeting someone else.

He went silently back to his Bells for a moment.

"James showed me your testing notes on that bottle that's been going around", he became more serious, "I'm impressed, very detailed", he continued, "It's all one ta' me, but you look like you know your stuff... got a bit of a *nose*".

I combined a look of modesty with annoyance, I could not avoid his appeal for conversation. "Just giving it time and some water", I declared.

He pointed to the upper shelf behind the bar, "You'll be int'a the malts next, The Bunna, the 'fiddich and the livit'", he chuckled, I gazed up at the small array of dust-glazed bottles of various shapes and styles set out sparingly along the narrow shelf, "I wuz a cooper myself for over thirty years", boasted Sanny, "Nevur missed a days work, evur, I could still clatter a cask together with my eyes shut", he boasted, he looked thoughtful for a moment, "listen", he said, "if your evur lookin' fur whiskies let me know, I sell stuff now and then", he winked.

James appeared behind the bar, "Ay Sanny", he nodded, neatly folding a dish towel over his shoulder, and after swiftly acknowledging his next customer standing patiently to our left he gathered some glasses and served some more drinks.

"Seriously", continued Sanny, "If your getting a taste for better stuff, I've got loads o' wee bottles in ma' garage, just sittin'", he leaned across the gap between us, lowering his voice slightly, "I will gi' you a mate's rate too, so it will'na put you out o' pocket", he mumbled.

I thanked him, finished my pint of No3, then with a passing wave to James, who was by this time now rushed off his feet with growing customer orders, I headed to the exit, and looking back for a moment as I released the door handle, I caught Sanny's eye, he winked then quickly looked back into his now empty glass.

It was a busy work-time for me, manager of a city centre restaurant with a constant influx of customers looking for anything from teas to steaks to cheesecakes. I had sixteen staff and good prospects to progress in catering but my heart was not in it, it was just not for me, it was simply a mis-matched career for me.

A few days later after a particularly hectic day at work, I headed back to the Smithy for a pint and found James in a surly mood, "Sanny", he snorted "that wee bastard's barred!, I willnae have glasses thrown around my bar", he shook his head, "And don't you get too involved wi' him, he's a cantankerous wee shite, *and,* that's when he's sober, he always drank too much during the day with that job of his".

I paused to allow James to vent-off, then gave him a further few minutes to finish washing some glasses before broaching a question, "So", I asked, "if he's not around here for a while, where will I find him for a few whisky samples?".

James glared, "As I said, you're better not getting involved with that one".

In the ensuing silence I sipped my pint, and engaged a different conversation, which seemed to work in bringing James back round from his recent bad experience. I could see he hated the violence which could occasionally enter a bar, it was personal to him, as if wanton violence had hurt him in his life, and badly, it was just a feeling I had about him, made visible by the fleeting anger in his moment of recall.

He cooled down, "Listen", he said in a manner to get my full attention, "Here's his number, and he lives just a few blocks down from here, but be sure you get him sober, so best time is in the morning, before ten, but not too early, mind".

A torn piece of beer mat was thrust towards me with the details.

The following morning was my one day in the week off work, and at nine thirty precisely I phoned Sanny's number. "Aye what 'yer want?", barked a woman's' voice down the line, "Er! Can I speak to Sanny please, I'm ralf, we met at his bar", the phone fell silent as feet shuffled off somewhere on the end of the line, then more silence, and more until eventually, after about five minutes a croaky trembling voice animated the receiver. "Wha' is it then, 'n why are you phoning at this time of the morning?", he grumbled.

"Hello Sanny, Ralfy here, I got your number from James and I know I can't see you there but you said you had some whisky for sale so I'm just phoning to see if it's still okay to follow-up!"

"Oh", he paused, " So I'm still barred... fick! it must be for a month then... fick!"

I remained silent to allow him to compose himself, now that it appeared that he fully realised the length of his sentence of banishment.

"Shite", he continued, "and I can't go tae tha' Fiddlurs or the Three Judges either, 'aw that's just pure shyte!" he concluded in clear exasperation.

I quickly took this opportunity to interject with my reason for the call. "You said you had wee bottles of malt for sale, how much and what have you got?"

One hour later, and a five minute bus ride, took me to the peeling-painted door of a basic functional council house in a less busy part of my neighbourhood. Sanny answered the door and lead me out across the weed-strewn garden to a rotting wooden garage supported on three sides by spindly conifer trees, which by default, appeared to be doing a remarkable job in holding up the structure of the shed.

With a swift tug he pulled up the aluminium single-swing door and disclosed an old Morris Minor car inside, surrounded by cardboard boxes of stuff. After a few seconds rummaging his way to the back of the place, he lifted out a medium sized plain box of assorted shape small bottles.

"Blenders samples", he declared, "Seemed a waste to fling them out, so my mate salvaged them off the skips!" he looked through the box contents intently, "I' gi'ye them fur ..." he paused with more than a passing look of guilt, "... twenty quid".

He went silent as if to anticipate my reaction.

"Okay", I said, "here you are!" I handed him a crisp new banknote and waited for him to hand me the box, he paused briefly surveying the back of the garage, obviously pleased at how quick the transaction had been agreed, and looked again at the crisp note in his hand, paused again then went to the back of the space returning with another smaller box of assorted bottles.

"Here", he said, "You can have this too as a wee extra".

It was clearly obvious that my lack of haggling or price-protesting had warmed his generosity.

With the two boxes in my hands, I returned on the bus to my flat and laid the contents out on the carpet in front of a fresh-lit coal fire for further examination. Most were clear 20cl bottles near-full or half empty with small sparse white paper labels stuck on. Brief ball-point hand written black ink notes were just visible on the labels, some so faded as to be almost indecipherable. I paused from gazing over what I had just bought and decided on a more methodical approach. Cup of tea first, and some buttered toast.

Kneeling on the carpet in front of the fire propped up on a couple of out-sized cushions, I picked up the nearest bottle standing in the cluster next to me. Macallan 1972 it said, 54.4% it continued, followed by what looked like a ball point pen initialled signature and a large tick. The second bottle label was similar, Highland Park 1941 40.3% it declared, this time the signature squiggle had a small cross next to it as if denoting a certain type of failure. All together there were around forty small assorted bottles in front of me and all with varying hues of amber, some almost black, some almost clear, some nearly full, some almost empty, and it was now going to be a long night of tastings.

Several tumblers were collected from the kitchen along with a small jug of tap water. I vividly remember the processions of silence over the hours, interrupted only by the gentle sigh of night wind passing my street-lighted windows, as the glow of coal fire met glow of poured whiskies transported on a cavalcade of successive smells and tastes, elevating my mindfulness slowly out of reality, and into a realm of pastoral, soft intoxication suffused with an ambient bliss which concluded eventually with falling asleep on the cushions in front of the fire around half past three in the morning.

When I woke I couldn't remember much about the smells and tastes as they had all blurred into one confusing and jumbled golden glow, followed laterally, by a memorably dry mouth and mildly sore head.

It was a start, and a good one too, I simply did not have the experience to understand how good and bad these samples were, there was so little point of reference, and no one to guide me who had already made the journey of discovery.

Sure enough, there's plenty who drink, millions drink, all the time, but far, far fewer stop and actually *taste*, simply slow down and *smell* and *taste* and ponder the alchemy of the experience.

To discover beauty we must first be aware in all our senses as to what beauty is, and what it actually, really means.

I walked brisky through the door of the bar (like a regular would) and hailed James the barman with a nod and wave. "No3 please James", I quipped, "And a wee goldy for Sanny if he's around anytime soon". James paused as the glass filled from the pump, he scowled, "You can save some cash there pal", he chided, "Sanny's barred again for winding up the punters, and I've had enough of him comin' in here pished in the afternoon", he paused for some dramatic effect, lowering his tone and slowing his words, "I cannae be seen serving irresponsibly, especially during the day when there's wumin around". I understood, seeing how the irascibility of Sanny when drunk would be an issue for other customers... especially women, who, I had noticed, he tended to over-stare at as and when they were in the vicinity.

Later, I phoned Sanny to follow up on the drama but he was not in the mood to talk and as he was clearly drunk, I quickly concluded my commiserations and hung up the receiver. I paused, reflecting on the inconvenience of alcoholism, all too common amongst those who worked in and around spirits, it made me frown, in my mind I changed the subject with myself, and headed into a licenced grocers around the corner from my street to buy a bottle of twelve year old Bunnahabhain. It came in a shorter round bottle, snug within a dark coloured cardboard tube with a metal pressed lid. The label showed a rugged, bonneted seafarer clutching a ship's wheel, whilst one hand shielded his eyes from what appeared to be a blustery sou'wester gale, and underneath was the inscription 'Westering Home'. How very appropriate for a malt from the Isle of Islay!

I never tire of opening the soft metallic seals of whisky bottles, the crisp zinc screw tops found mainly with blended scotch bottles offer a satisfyingly dry 'crack' as they break, but it is the theatre of soft cork stoppers in malt bottles that provides such engaging theatrical anticipation as to the contents. These metal seals are soft and silent, ripping quietly a full three hundred and sixty degrees around the bottle neck, circumnavigating the aperture before pulling away to reveal the un-sealing which is so irreversible. The remaining soft metal sleeve pulls away like silk and the first tug of the short, soft cork of the stopper can be now engaged.

'Pop', loud and aquatic, echoing up and out of the glass neck, dragging out the first aroma of malt-complexity which stimulates the soul and fuels great expectations; -

…so distinctive,

…so melodic,

…so affirmative,

…so absolute,

…so wondrous!

I hurried into the Bar later than I normally would, anticipating James's interest and applause over a No3 as I would recount how a teaspoon of 'Bunna' in a glass of 'Islander' would *lift* and *complify* the glass of cheaper blended, but the expression on his face behind the bar lowered the conviviality of my greeting. He looked sad and slightly guilty, the dish towel wound tightly round his hand like a rosary, "Sorry pal", he paused, looking across the room, "Sanny's died... he fell in his garage, sorting his boxes", James paused to regain his composure, "Fell and banged his head, poor wee bastard".

Sanny's funeral was a low-key and a quiet affair. His widow was quite calm about the ceremony, smoking cigarettes at every opportunity whilst waiting for a nod from the undertaker for departure from the Parlour.

The cortege left from from the door of Robertson's Funeral Service in Hayburn Street, a small and oddly quiet cortege of hearse along with a mis-matching limousine, which then proceeded down Dumbarton Road to Clydebank Crematorium, situated just above Auchentoshan Distillery at North Dalnottar. I watched the procession depart from the corner of Dumbarton Road as it made it's way out and along the congested main street.

The solitary flowers inside of the hearse resting at the head of the coffin were small, nothing more than a well-wisher's bouquet of spindly red and white carnations carelessly contained within pink plastic wrapping featuring pink cartoon balloons and ribbons. There was no attached message card.

About three weeks later James pushed a small grubby piece of folded paper towards me as I perused my first pint of the evening.

"Ella asked me to get you to give her a call".

"Who's Ella?" I asked curiously.

"Sanny's wife", retorted James. "She's still, well, sort-of upset, what with Sanny gone and leaving her with an unpaid house and all... at least give her a phone anyway. She is very keen that I get you to get in touch", he concluded.

I was curious, I gave her a phone call later that night.

"Awww! Thanks Son fur' gettin' back, it's so much appreciated what with me suffering ma' loss", she gushed, "Am' just sayin' tae m'self, that Ralfy's an awful nice boy and Sanny liked you too. Would you come down tae the hoose tomorrow and pick up a box of whiskies he wanted you tae huv'?"

It was bright, blustery, cold and sunny, clouds scurried across a shifting sky as I got off the bus by Sanny's house, I shivered at how so much had changed since my last, but recent visit.

Ella answered the door too quickly as I rang the bell, now smartly dressed and reeking of perfume, "It's 'affy good of you tae' get here so quick an' all, I'm in an awful state, what with the loss and such".

She breezed me round to the garage. Inside the floor was spotless, recently swept, mopped and rinsed thoroughly, the car had been moved.

She beckoned me towards a large, strong box in the corner, it contained about a dozen or so assorted bottles of single malts, all in pristine condition along with a couple of blue blenders glasses and an ornate water jug.

"He wanted you tae' have them son", she quipped, lighting up another cigarette and looking earnestly into my face as if to better gauge my reaction. "They're free for you, he seemed to take a shine to you son, which wisnae like him... really!" she added, curious and suspicious at the same time, then thoughtfully concluding, "He wasna' what you'd call a *people person*. Mind you though, I put two extra bottles in the box tae fill it up, and they will have to cost you", she paused as if to recalibrate her price, "... forty pounds, but they're all full up and sealed as you can see", she pointed, her cigarette ash tumbling into the box.

I was completely on the spot here, it all seemed so surreal, I couldn't marshall my thoughts whilst thinking of a response so I simply agreed. "There you are then Ella, thanks", I handed across two twenty pound notes.

She grabbed them quickly from my hand.

As we passed a still burning brazier behind the front gate, Ella paused, the heat was still intense although the flames had long since diminished, "Shame to see it all go", she mused, then after a pause to allow some welling emotions to settle back down, she lifted a garden cane and stirred the residual embers, "He loved his poetry you know", she declared, "Books and books of the stuff, nice and neatly written too", she shivered, "But now it's all burnt so no one will have to bother reading it", she concluded, seemingly pleased almost to have removed a little bit more of Sanny from her life.

Back at my flat, all was quiet, both arms were slowly recovering from the excessive weight of all the bottles in one box, 14 to be exact, now that I had time to check them over on the bus back.

With the assistance of a fresh brewed and hot cup of tea, I sorted through the contents. Talisker 10yo, Auchentoshan 21yo, Macallan 18yo, Royal Salute 21yo, and two blue cobalt coloured sniffing glasses along with a ceramic water jug. My collection had begun, my horizons were expanding.

That very same week I was issued along with all my staff with redundancy notices. The restaurant was now in profit so could be sold as a successful business, but not as a restaurant.

Three months later I began a new career as a Trainee Funeral Director with the Co-operative Society. It all happened so fast.

Chapter Three

Discovering Malt-Moments

On Location

Notes.
Exotic variety of nostalgic flavours, creamy, savoury, some-times sour and occasionally some bitterness but with an original substance of character which delivers a memorable experience to the senses over time. Needs a bit of water!

I'm having trouble with a particular malt and not for the first time.

I have just opened the bottle, and immediately I notice, on first nosing, that something is wrong, just *wrong*, but it's not so much that the malt is particularly bad, it's just that it's less-good compared to the last bottle I bought which was not that long ago.

I am left to puzzle about why this is.

It's raining again, in a very wetting, Glasgow way, a heady combination of cold seeping dampness, gray tones, and aggressive chill, which is something about Glasgow that I never get used to although, in truth I love this city dearly.

As soon as I moved to Glasgow from my original home located less fortuitously south west of the compact Victorian city, I imme-diately felt at home in a way I could not initially explain or fully understand.

The weather was the main instigator for opening up the fireplace in the compact front room of my top-floor flat in Gardner Street, Partick, which had been blocked some years previously by the last owner with an old woollen bed blanket.

The flat is described locally as a 'single-end', and is very typical of this lowly working area, adjacent to derelict shipyards, shabby shops, and a post-industrial age grubbiness which, on better acquaintance, and with growing familiarity, provides a certain charm and characterful presence.

It took a while to pull the blackened tatty wool blanket from out of the chimney stack, as it had been pushed well into the vent to exclude drafts, and as the material came free from the stack, a hefty cloud of soot and skeletal bird-remains descended into the hearth with an aroma of stale old coal, savoury tar and musty ozone. The vacuum cleaner made short work of the pile of blackened residue and soon I was able to confirm, with the assistance of some burning newspaper, that the up-draft within the fireplace chimney was strong and steady. Coal was delivered, sticks for tinder were collected, matches were on stand-by and I was ready to instigate the perfect accompaniment for a dram of whisky, a living, burning, glowing, dancing, crackling, hissing, warming, iridescent wood and coal fire.

With the lights low in the evening, and the hostility of the wintery weather rattling against my slowly rotting sash windows, I would draw my curtains across sealing off the outward troubling world and settle with an assortment of bottles in front of the cheery ever-animated flame-enriched fire to savour the warmth, both inside of me, and out.

Whisky is *warming,* more so than bourbon or rum, for the simple reason that it is made and then drunk in a cold country, noted for long dark days, and with winters that keep the nights longer than they should be.

'Siberia-by-the-sea', as we locals hate-lovingly refer to Scotland as when sharing out sentiments of home.

The sensation is simple, the liquor is nosed, affirmed as aromatic and pleasant, then the liquor is sipped slowly, a wee drop at a time and then perhaps a bigger drop as the tastes become more familiar and are thereafter enjoyed at a steady, but not too hasty a pace, until the glass is empty and ready to be refilled yet again to further sustain the mood of the moment.

I am lost in realms of amber haze infused both with original thoughts and suffused by subtle less-known moods, in an air around me which hangs thick with wispy outlines of fleeting ghosts along with teasing sprites, who weave such ethereal visions for contemplation that my very soul is elevated on the beating wings of discovered inspiration, driven on by intermitant waves of faltering intoxication, as like the eternal churning waves by a waters edge on twilight beaches, nursed by the restless and deep oceans of feelings and awareness.

Such it is to be human, and to live, and to notice such things.

That's the theory anyway, and right enough, this is more often the case, however, a bad whisky can damage the mood and that is what is happening to me tonight with this bottle of malt.

I seem to be getting the hang of drinking whisky, Sanny's well-timed intervention sent me on a trail of discovery with many cask samples in small bottles, but now they are all gone save for some tired old Highland Park well past its best.

I am buying retailer bottles now, and have been for the last six months, Bunnahabhain, Glenfiddich, Glenfarclas, Glenlivet, Macallan, Auchentoshan etc, many bottles opened fairly quickly but thereafter slow to empty, and rarely finished completely.

This is the moment in which I begin to notice how a whisky will change shape, form and flavour as the fill-level goes down over time, with it starting at de-corking as more woody, raw-ish, malty, grainy and slightly harsh, thereafter transubstantiating with exposure to air over time into spicier, softer, barley-sugared, gentler and aromatic enhancement from its former self, to softer glory. Glenfiddich less so, Glenfarclas more so.

This particular malt is pissing me off, I don't have the experience yet to fully understand what the problem is, why there's a difference, an issue, a reason for protest.

I will find out why!

I need to know.

Unexpectedly, and as a direct result of being made redundant along with sixteen other members of staff from the restaurant I ran for two years, I have now had to find fresh employment.

The regional manager responsible for the restaurant apologises sincerely and I think he is sincere.

He assures us that we will all get good references, and sticks to his word, so everybody goes onto better paying and more rewarding jobs if they really want to. I have to wait three months and endure some dead-end job interviews with hospitals, jewellers, institutional caterers and 'job-matching' consultants, which is a total waste of time, and a very uncomfortable experience.

Then with patience, fortitude, and luck, a job appears, it's the ultimate dead-end job with prospects.

In December 1988 I become a Trainee Funeral Director with the Glasgow Co-operative Funeral Service. This job would change my outlook on life permanently.

Long hours are required with it being a service industry, and as it is an interesting job with no two days the same, I accepted the sacrifice of precious time and in doing so, double my income due to overtime payments.

Now!... something you need to know malt-mates, I hate banks, because I know what they actually are, more specifically, I hate the usury which banking imposes on the masses, and which stagnates social evolution and creative development.

Lets talk about mortgages for a minute, I needed one when I bought my flat and watched as the bank bureaucrat along with the conveyancer and estate agent, shoe-horned into my very modest mortgage allocation preset time restrictions, short-term loans with extortionate interest, along with a deceitful endowment policy that I asked NOT to have. I will never forget, nor forgive, the brazen usury and inhumanity of this system and the people who enable it.

This is the reason I have never spent money I don't have, have shunned credit, have refused all banking 'investment' products and refuse to borrow... and I just want to take this opportunity to tell you that 'Mortgage' is made up using two latin words, 'Mort' (death) and 'gage' (grip).

Words on their own can carry powerful messages.

I mention the bank *thing* simply to introduce to you what I did next.. I bought whisky, lots and lots of it, in fact my purchasing became obsessive, and over the next two years I had a collection of two hundred and fifty unopened bottles. All sorts, all brands, all ages and all flavours.

This required time, money and effort, and along with my Industry-working contacts in the local bars, I took to visiting specialist whisky shops around Glasgow on the malt-hunt.

Starting locally, I bought generic high-street stuff but on discovering Peckhams the licenced Deli and Oddbins my range of options rocketed. One thing I did discover early on was the lack of knowledge and whisky experience in most shops. Quality? They would respond, well that's Macallan, it's very *Smooth,* and it has the reputation. It's the best one, always!

I had tried Macallan several times in bars and out of my own bottles, sure it was good, but not *that* good.

I was up on Great Western Road, and on passing the grubby, cracked window of a dusty off-licence liquorist newsagent, I spotted some classy black, gold and cream boxes of whisky marked with names like Brora, Port Ellen, Clynelish, Bladnoch, Glen Ord and Teaninich. At around seventy five pounds each, they were considered expensive for a high-strength, older-aged single malt, but I shuffled into the dimly lit premises and was met by a motionless man reading a newspaper spread out on the counter.

He barely glanced up, "Yass?" he asked, "Whaa' you wan'?"

I indicated to the whiskies in the window, "Can I have one of each box of all the range", I asked.

He blinked, paused, looking at me more directly and for longer this time, and removed eight boxes of whisky from the shelves, with the resultant gaps created, allowing the outside sunlight to animate the interior of the shop a bit more. He counted the bottles again then counted the cost. " Can you tell me much about the boxes?" I enquired, "No, not really, it's alcohol isn't it", he stated bluntly, I paused awaiting the final tally " Six hundred and ten pounds and two pence", he concluded, his mood brightening considerably.

I placed the crisp twenty pound notes neatly in a tidy bundle on

the counter and laid a tenner and two penny piece on top of them...
He almost smiled.

I never went back.

I had a lot more luck at Oddbins, in the more gentile retail environment of the Crow Road shop, a bright, recently redecorated, and more modern retail set-up with a mock pot-still sitting in the corner surrounded by high and fancy shiny wooden display cases broadcasting bottles of expensive stuff sitting under small intense spot lights, which gave the area a nice warmth. I liked it.

They offered me some free samples in a proper nosing glass.

I liked it.

The staff there were much more enthused about whisky than I had encountered anywhere else.

I liked it too.

I liked it so much that I started to spend more cash, lots of cash. It was my hobby after all, and I did not have a car to run, home-improvements to finance, or a family to drain my resources.

After all, I was an undertaker and saw first hand on many occasions, how much damage families can do to one another primarily to comply with social 'norms'.

I was having a slow and methodical scan along the shelves behind the lengthy counter, wandering past the pyramid stacks of carelessly piled cases of assorted wines, intermittently punctuated with isolated cases and bottles of less-known aperitifs, liqueurs and tonics, when I suddenly spotted the Port Ellen, an official bottling tucked discreetly away on a shelf less-visible from the till. A voice to my right intervened in a light, cheery tone, "Amaaa-zing stuff, great, really good peating levels, we've only got six in the store, so's it's one per customer he he he he".

I looked round to see a tousle-headed, young, bespectacled chap in a hand knitted greenish woolly jumper, grinning, "We've only got six in the store", he repeated as if affirming to himself that this particular whisky was of *such* noteworthy status that only six bottles were available to sell in one specialist shop which was clearly a very unusual situation and merited comment even where the customer was still looking, but not yet buying.

31

"So, I can only sell you one bottle", he concluded, staring intently towards me, earnestly gaging my reaction. I kept my poker face, "Oh!", I bluffed, "I suppose I'd better buy a bottle before you run out".

He fetched a small set of steps, and soon had a dignified dark plain cardboard box with an off-white label in his hand. Port Ellen, it read, 56.2%vol: "Really unusual", he quipped, "releasing so little at one time when there seems to be a bit of demand now the distilleries shut down and become a maltings"... he clearly knew his stuff.

As if suddenly remembering something trivial but important, he turned to me asking, "Are you a drinker or collector?" I looked confused at this seemingly erroneous question, "Er, drinker, it's for drinking, but not just yet, probably later, it's just that it's different"

He leaned across the counter lowering his voice, "I'm an Ileach... from Islay", he paused, "I prefer Bruichladdich, that's my distillery but I suppose I like them all eventually, really", he concluded ruefully.

"I'm Andy by the way, Andy Bell, pleased to meet you, would you like a dram?" he asked, pulling out an opened bottle of the Port Ellen from under the counter.

I nodded, and let him pour a generous portion into a proper copita nosing glass.

Water was added.

I nosed it,

paused,

tasted it,

paused,

added another small drop of water,

paused,

tasted it again lingering on the aftertaste.

Andy looked on approvingly, as if applauding the habits of a proper whisky drinker, I looked up from my glass, "Just curious", I said, "why ask if I'm collecting or drinking, after all, I could be doing both?, and by the way", I continued, "Do you have much to do with Talisker at all?"

I paused, engaging Andy intently for a suitable response, he thought for a moment, "Peppery, ginger and decent peating levels, but I prefer the Islay malts, but if I'm offered it, I won't say no, generally I would say it's fine, not had a bad one really", he paused, looking into the middle distance as if prompting the better memory of a less acquainted dram, a few seconds later and the subject seemed to be concluded in his view.

He leaned further across the counter, "You would be surprised about how many people are now collecting this stuff", he tapped the bottle with his pen making it ring slightly, "Not even interested in drinking it... unbelievable", he concluded, "If the bottle label or box is at all damaged a collector won't touch it, they want every bottle *perfect,* the drinkers don't mind a wee scratch, squint label, bashed box etc, but collectors can be so damn fussy, but I suppose that's life".

"That's life", I agreed, enjoying the sudden philosophy.

Andy frowned, contemplating an invisible but important consideration, "Listen", he said, "I've seen you around a few times in the shop and you seem to know your stuff, are you interested in buying a ticket for a whisky tasting evening next week?"

"Yup, sold, two tickets please if you have them!"

It was a 'B' name single malt extravaganza.

The following week, a work friend from the Co-operative and I sat round a bench table with about twenty other whisky enthusiasts, and sampled our way through five single malts as provided by Andy, who was hosting the evening.

Several Balvenie's and several Bruichladdich's were all savoured 'responsibly' after which Andy pulled a final dram out the bag for us all to try, one we had not yet encountered, Brora, and an official bottling of a new thirty year old version, first release, 52.4% alcohol.

It was stunningly good, leaving all malts before, and many later, to be shaded in it's memory-glow.

You see, that's the problem with discovering the *best,* is that the rest, before and after, diminish a little from the new experience.

That is just the way it is, appreciating whisky and other fine spirits from around the world is a law of diminishing returns over time, and it does take time, and sure, there are always some wonderful new experiences in smell and taste to be discovered, often by accident, or by anorak persistence in the search for malt-moments but they are forever in the memory shadow of the outstandingly great whiskies, both single malt and occasionally blended scotch.

It's not only the un-erasable memory forged from smell and taste over time, two of our most subjective and instinctive senses, which leave powerful signals of recollection in our mind's archives, but also, those rare moments of exotic location and sometimes those most colourful of people who have shared our malt-moments, which then weave such brighter threads into the rich tapestry of our lives.

We are honoured to have experienced them and privileged to have shared them.

So often it is the human condition to undervalue the most valuable of things in life due to our own foolishness and the presence of social and environmental pressures.

From three different shops I bought three different bottles of Brora 30 year old 1st Edition.

The cost blew my budget for two months!

Sourcing for my increasingly hoarded collection of bottles took me further and further away from Glasgow.

When in Edinburgh, I would spend time in three frequently rewarding locations, Cadenheads at the foot of the Royal Mile, where a well-aged bottle-green door would open into a rather cramped, box-cluttered antiquated space which was dominated, on the right-hand wall by several large blackboards listing in alphabetical order all the varieties, ages and alcoholic strengths of malts, blends and other spirits for sale at that moment in time.

Being primarily single cask and cask strength bottlings, the turnover of names of distilleries on the boards over time was considerable and many distillery names would have a small tombstone marked R.I.P. on them to designate the fact that that distillery was now either moth balled or demolished, and definitely no longer producing whisky.

My other favourite Edinburgh shop, and it still is, was Royal

Mile Whiskies at the top of the Royal Mile opposite St Giles Cathedral.

Staff there were young, enthusiastic, educated and willing to spend time talking to and listening to a 'whisky anorak.'

A few words of explanation here readers – anoraks are cheap warm functional jackets with hoods worn by obsessive enthusiasts, entertainingly autistic about their selected passion, train-spotting, coin collecting, whisky drinking etc. The 'anorak' application denotes non-standard obsessive people.

The availability of far less known independent bottlings from a tremendous range of whisky bottlers including Signatory, Adelphi and Gordon & MacPhail was excellent.

I found that buying these Independent bottler whiskies seemed to offer a *fresher,* more characterful and flavoursome alternative to official Distillery bottlings, and usually a bit cheaper too.

My third port of call in Edinburgh was Raeburn Wines which was situated near to Edinburgh Botanic Gardens, and along with a very discerning selection of wines, sold its own Independent bottlings of malts under the name 'The Bottlers'. I bought quite a few of these beauties and never had a bad experience.

Another useful whisky-location source was the Green Welly Stop on the A82 road heading north past Loch Lomond near Crianlarich. Staff were a lot less knowledgable, and on my occasional visits to buy stuff, seemed entertained by my eclectic choices and the money I was spending.

I didn't care anyhow as it was, after all, a glorious obsession coupled with a good day out!

One of the best shops I visited was a bit of a distance to travel, in fact almost a full day away from home but the journey in my little car was filled with quiet roads and charming highland scenery, from Loch Lomond around to Lochgilphead, stopping off for pie and coffee at Inveraray, home to a small but colourful specialist whisky shop called Loch Fyne Whiskies.

As soon as I walked through the door of this converted terraced cottage, I fell in love with the place and it's engaging characters. Andy, the affable, moustached whisky communicator whose natural manner and enthusiasm could sell sand to Arabia, and there was Laura too, a mature, refined and genteel lady whose greying hair and matching dresses added yet more class to her presence. Richard was the boss, a tall, tousle headed, pudding-faced cheer-meister of a typically British eccentric disposition who spent most of his time trying to hide, unsuccessfully, in the corner hunched over a laptop attending to on-line purchases and sales in between drinking more coffee. Of all the retailers I have ever been in, Loch Fyne Whiskies, as it was in the 1990s was the best in terms of stock range along with honest, informed, experienced and friendly staff.

Laura gave me a friendly wink as I entered Loch Fyne Whiskies, "Och! it's yourself again, seems like yesterday when you were last in", she grins. It has in fact been three weeks, and on the last visit I bought eight bottles and spent five hundred pounds.

Today I will spend more and buy more, as it's an itching obsession, and I'm better with bottles than a bank balance.

Within a couple of minutes, during which I swiftly scan around the packed shelves for new stuff, or exciting stuff with higher prices, Laura calls over from the broad front counter, "Can we offer you a wee dram while you're here?"

I accept without asking what is being offered, whatever it is it will very good, the samples here always are. I nurse the offered miniature Glencairn tumbler in my hand, sherried, fruity, woody and complex, "Twenty one year old Glenfarclas", she says, "recent batches have been very good, I really like the sherried whiskies myself", she muses.

I buy two bottles.

Andy shuffles round the corner, gingerly navigating along the floor-to-ceiling precarious stacks of malts, "Have you tried that new Compass Box thing", he asks, "New thing, some guy, ex-Diageo, American, names John, John, Joh... aw shite, I cannae remember his name, nevur mind, try a wee taster anyway", I do, it's delicious, I buy a bottle.

It's blended Scotch, called Asyla, very tasteful packaging, I'm very impressed at the obvious attention to detail, not typical of Scotch at all. Yet another Indi: bottler pops up on my radar, and the bottling strength is higher than normal too!

The bottles and their boxes, as supplied, soon stack up on the counter, Richard pops his head round from behind a display case and offers a cheerful salute, "They call me Mr Fish you know", he states, then disappears back behind the display to see who has sent an e-mail or an order, or both, or nothing.

I return to the stash of seven bottles in need of payment, as they stand, clustered together into a strong cardboard box. "That will be four hundred and twenty two pounds please, Ralfy", Laura says as the till spits out the itemised receipt, I pay with cash and while she counts the notes I extend my malt-moment chat with Andy covering smoky peat monsters, chill filtration, added caramel colouring, and other potential hazards that can compromise a good whisky.

Timing is perfect , and as I head with my box to the door, a troop of Scandinavians enter wrapped in rain-proof clothing colourful and functional. They civilly hold the door open for me to exit, and with the mass of people still outside waiting to enter I appreciate I have missed another busy moment which would have compromised the quality of my experience at Loch Fyne.

I have never liked whisky shops when they are too busy, it spoils the magic.

After an earlier experience in Inveraray, when I could barely move in the shop because of a recently decanted tourist bus full of slow, elderly people, looking too long at what they had no intention of buying, or understanding.

I made a point of timing visits carefully between bus parties and this of course meant that with more time, and growing acquaintance, I was offered more samples of better stuff. A pub lunch of soup and steak pie at the George Hotel across the road and concluding with a strong coffee, plus a longish walk around the village, set me up nicely for the drive home.

It's on the drive back home as I first catch sight of Loch Lomond at Tarbet that I have a sudden and slightly shocking idea!... that's what's wrong with my angry malt, the reason I am not enjoying it so much, it's chill filtered, has added E150a colourant and to top it off, a very boring box and a label that looks like it was designed by a bored accountant!

When I arrive home, just as darkness has finally fallen, the box of treasures is dumped on the front room floor by the fireside and after putting on the kettle for a cuppa I pull out the offending malt, right enough, about 46% vol alcohol, good! More flavour. A jaffa-orange glow of amber denoting caramel E150a colourant, and on pouring a glass and adding a little water, no 'scotch mist' delivered from the haze of barley oils and cask extract. Then with a sudden awakening I realise how commercial processing can lessen a whisky, diminish it and bring it down, then to add to that, any presence of bad quality cask influences compound this problem. Suddenly, armed with this knowledge I feel cheated, but also, as if I have reached a mile-stone in my understanding and knowledge of whisky.

I get my rapidly cooling cup of tea from the kitchen, and squatting down on the carpet in front of my now glowing fire crackling away in the open hearth, I examine the box and bottle of problematic malt again. It is a rather boring lack-lustre box.

I try another glass, smelling, tasting, frowning.

I put it aside and pour two other drams, some Glenfarclas and some Glen Elgin, both are excellent, full-flavoured, 'rounded' aromatic, complex and they just *feel* affirmative for what they are!

I go back to the bad malt, nope, no way, it's simply around twenty percent short of what it should be and I am not a happy 'bunny'!

I re-register the need to know further about what's wrong with this malt.

I know that compared to the little sips my father offered me as a teenager many years previously I had encountered a fruitier, more peppery, *rich* malt which, although too young and inexperienced, I 'got' what was going on in the glass then. Now it's different, and more than the chill filtering, more than the additional colourant added to cosmetically enhance the appearance of the product because most people are daft enough to believe that darker colour means better flavour... try Loch Dhu and prepare for a shock!

True, on adding a little drop of the Glenfarclas to the offensive malt, it did over the next few hours improve it greatly.

Four weeks later, and a month nearer to summertime, I drive north via Fort William to Mallaig and take a neat and characterful Cal Mac ferry over the scenic waters to charming and cosy Armadale, thereafter heading up a windy and distinctly crumbling road towards a small settlement called Sligachan, after which the smaller, crumbling road leads westwards over bleak sharded hills to meet the encroaching Atlantic Ocean near Carbost at Loch Harport. Whatever they tell you, the real reason that there was traditionally only one distillery on the Isle Of Skye has a lot to do with politics.

Skye is a 'separate' place in Scotland, it has a different feel, different people haunted by clan brutalities and family vendettas remembering back hundreds of years or longer, when the people are mindful of it, which they are, often.

It's fine, If you visit Skye temporarily for scenery and the fishing, you're sorted. Different if you stay there like I did a few years previously, working at a country hotel for three months doing a summer job which often felt like confinement in a concentration camp, filled with peculiar people doing dysfunctional things.

The distillery is tidy, neat and a whitewashed scattering of buildings containing five well groomed stills, the neatly-presented lady who provides the tour is engaging and professional but also careful in her response to my increasingly specific questions as we shuffle round the pre-designated tour route. "NO photos in the still room", she announces loudly as we enter into the heart of production. I'm baffled, "Why not?" I ask, "Because the flash off your camera might ignite alcohol fumes in the air", she responds.

I don't bother asking any more questions after that except for "Where are the warehouses with all the casks?" She responds breezily as if glad this particular tour is coming to a conclusion, "All our new-make spirit is taken by tanker to Perth where it is better monitored for maturation."

"Oh!... er, thanks for that", I reply, I am not impressed, already I recognise that divorcing a barley spirit from it's place of make disrupts the authenticity and provenance of the liquor, and its flavour, and it's function.

That night I park my car in a clearing not far from the distillery, and as night falls I wander back and around the outside to get a better feel for what it's all about. I find myself slightly sad as there is clearly a *silence* over the place, despite the noise of activity, and hum of production that gets even louder as I pick up on the lack of people, thinness of community, and that certain emptiness that corporate activity brings to commerce.

It seems as if the very soul of this distillery is suspended until further notice.

The following morning after having slept in the back of my car like a log, thanks to quarter of a bottle of ten year old Talisker, I drive back the way I came, wiser, more informed, more aware of scotch whisky than ever before, and glad to be heading back to Glasgow where it's just *warmer* despite the consistently cool weather of cloud and rain that keeps the country green, wet and 'dreech' (wet and miserable).

The climate here is the reason that firesides are such a welcome accompaniment to whisky, a living fire transmits life and energy into a room which compliments a glass of whisky so incredibly well, a perfect partnership of cheer and positivity, so long as both are respected.

The following day I walk down Dumbarton Road to Oddbins for a catch-up with Andy Bell, an exchange of malt-info, and some crake Cheery and as welcoming as always, he has an idea to share. I keep quiet for now and listen up, "Just found out there's a whisky club started in the city centre, I'm thinking of going along, are you interested in checking it out, I think it could be fun", he chirps!

Chapter Four

The Undertakers Stash!

Notes.
A growing arrival of maturity primarily from assorted casks which compliment the fresh-fruit nature of the spirit perfectly. Some bitter note in development but still one to savour and give extra time to enjoy. Loving the colour.

The rain was late in the day, perhaps a sign of the growing daylight hours as summer filled the city with more light though not a lot more sunshine. March gave way to April and I had not yet finished my last bought bottle of single malt.

It was my only bottle of malt whisky where I would add ice into a tumbler, a cut glass heavy-based thing with a thistle on it, and a distant mountain etched into the surface. However I don't approve of malts being used for 'cocktails' too often, so was also sipping Glenfarclas long and slow from a recently acquired Glencairn glass, an ideal receptacle for the job of drammin'.

Fortunately, due to my ongoing irrational commitment and good resourcing, I now had twenty two opened bottles to choose from and some were quite good, others very good, none were bad.

All were better than the one bad malt.

It remained unloved, but taught me a lot.

The rain finally arrived again. I looked out my upstairs flat front window and watched the little frothy rivers of falling water gurgle and flow along the roadside, and into square iron drains, disappearing out of view on their brisk way underground and down to the

River Clyde. 'If I go out now', I thought, 'I will need my welly boots on and a rain jacket', I mused to myself as this was all the endorsement I needed to make a decision, so put on the rain gear and went down to the Smiddy for a pint of No:3.

It was busy inside as I shook off the wet from my coat and entered the pub which, as I now knew it and it's characters for three years, seemed like a familiar and reliable second home. The hubbub of conversation along with clinking of assorted glasses all enveloped within a brown and grey threaded cloud of cigarette smoke enveloped me, all was well, cosy and rosy till I caught sight of James behind the bar.

"I'm leaving", he said, "I'm going to call it a day with the Smiddy, there's new owners and they want to change the customers for higher spenders". He sighed, looking to the ceiling as if for further explanation, "It's been five years and I will miss the place, but I know the writings on the wall with this place... it's not going to survive as it is".

I bought my pint of No3 and gave it a moments silence before replying, I reflected for a moment and changed completely what I was about to say, "I will miss you and this place, but only as I knew it, so I can't come back again, it would not be the same...", my voiced trailed off as if concluding my statement with more self-reflection.

James brightened up, "They won't be selling so many malts now at the weekend, just not popular, too old fashioned", he paused, then abruptly changed the subject, "My son does that Muay Thai boxing", he paused again to guage my reaction, "Got quite good over the last year, competing in Thailand now", I looked across the bar, impressed with the boy's progress. James rested both elbows onto the bar and leaned across lowering his voice a little so as not to broadcast. "We are selling the flat soon, and then moving to somewhere near Bangkok", he looked across the room into the middle distance caught up in his own imagination and dreams, "The missus and I are opening a bar, the boy will train and work with us, I *feel* in myself it's the right thing to do now".

I nodded in support of his plan, drank up quickly, gave James a wave as I went to leave, then returned and shook his hand properly, holding for a few extra seconds, "All the best mate, thanks for the drams and chats... good luck".

As I left through the outside door of the bar, familiar and atmospherically tactile as it was through the last few years of going in and out, and chatting, buying bottles, and sharing whisky gossip, and loving it all, I was suddenly gripped by a complex pang of nostalgia.

As I stood at the exit, the slow and measured swing-shut of the heavy door briefly colluded to mix smoky bar warmth and ambient electric light infused with communal chatter into the outside. Chilly, fresh, wet air carried briskly on the intense breeze of yet another windy high-street squall, driving the spattering uninvited drops of heavy rain diagonally into my face.

I was silhouetted now in a monochrome night-kissed evening, lit with orangey streetlight and animated busy shoppers.

Pulling up my collar for protection against the sudden elements I briefly, for just a second, could have sworn that the ghost of Sanny the cooper shuffled drunkenly past me and in through the now almost closed door.

Emotions of bitter sweet nostalgia for auld lang syne tumbled across my mind, as turbulent and distracting as the cloud strewn rain now getting heavier and wetter within the encroaching night.

I shivered at the strangeness of the feelings and headed briskly up Gardner Street to my flat for a hot cup of tea followed by a cool glass of whisky.

This is just the way life is, we make plans and plans are made for us by the three fates, those mythological ladies who roll their dice of happenstance that mere mortals, and even the ancient gods, are bound by the truth of their imposed reality.

It's no wonder we have a drink now and then.

I put on the kettle, light the fire and pour a couple of drams on the mantlepiece as the stew begins to simmer on the stove in the kitchen. Lamb stew, beans and potatoes, seasoned with thyme and garlic, cannae beat it.

An early lesson learned in the appreciation of whisky is that liquor is all the more satisfying if one has a full stomach after a tasty meal, and one also gets mildly pished a lot more slowly too.

I place a full pint of fresh tap water with the glasses of whisky and leave them to air as I scoff my dinner. These cold nights need warming meals.

I strategically prop up a couple of comfy cushions on the carpet in front of the hearth and settle down to an ambient evening of malt-moments... and they are not long in arriving.

Port Ellen from Gordon and MacPhail, an official single cask Knockdhu, and a Cadenhead version of Glen Grant round off the tryptic with all of them matured well over twenty years in their assorted casks.

I mull over the sense of age that I can smell and taste, it is sublime, ethereal, deep and resonating within my consciousness.

I am aware of a light connect to my subconsciousness which displays itself in soft and complex emotions which drift back and forth on waves of alcohol-inspired contemplation. The presence of original thoughts and deeper resonance is palpable. I drift on the amber air of contentment and appreciate the presence of a wonderful companion... silence!

Silence is so often misunderstood and dismissed within an overactive world.

To most people the sound of silence is nothing more than the absence of noise, a sort of 'quiet' and 'in between noises' thing with no substance or form, however I know better.

Orlando the orange cat mentioned this many years previously in a passing conversation we exchanged in the garden. Cats, you see, *know* what silence really is, it's NOT the absence of sound by the replacement of noise with the presence of audible soundlessness.

Orlando, like all cats, loved the presence of silence and was always comfortable with it.

The African philosopher Abel Amozewe put it very well when he said in 1820 that, "I summon silence to be my friend, he is my companion and we talk in silence and listen in silence with our conversations... he listens well and understands the planet well, the earth, the sky, the seas, the air, he is always listening and understanding and teaching me about the universe and all that is in it". He concludes, "Silence, he knows that I am just a child and has great patience with me when I am troubled".

I totally agree with Abel, he really got it right, and inspired by the muse of whiskies over the years I have got to know silence even better, for ours is a most rewarding friendship indeed. Original thoughts and inspirational ideas along with sudden deep knowledge have always marked our conversation..

Orlando the orange cat is now purring loudly, stretching slowly now and again and is curled up by the flickering fire, which is really just a little bit strange as he has been dead for fifteen years.

I ignore the disturbing logic of my thoughts and decide not to worry about it, leaving him be whilst sleepiness creeps slowly towards me across the carpet, over the cushions, and into my fussy fussy head where I spiral into sleep perchance to dream of cats and silence and whiskies and tomorrow and tomorrow and tomorrow...

The following day is a work day, an early start with a loud, clattering alarm call from my clock.

All my whisky glasses and water jug are empty although all the liquor bottles still have plenty of content. Orlando is no longer around, having gone with the mellow, and at times surreal mood of the malts from the night before.

I quite like my job. I am suited to it. It happened by accident because life just happens to be full of accidents, but most of the time we just don't notice them because were getting on with life under the illusion that conventional decisions are always important.

I started as a trainee funeral director with the Co-operative Funeral Service in 1988. Glasgow, and where I was based in Scotland Street was the largest single provision hub in the nation-wide business and as such was far larger in scale than most locally based undertakers which might have one or two hearses. In Glasgow, providing for seventy five percent of the city's population, we had fourteen hearses, with two more on standby if needed at busy times. There were thirty two full time funeral directors, five managers, thirty limousine drivers and twenty one arrangers situated in local neighbourhood parlours scattered throughout the City. There was a lot to learn, and quickly, with arrangement making, both burial and cremation, driving large public vehicles including private ambulance vans, communicating diplomatically with very upset people, and some not so upset, and then there was the memorising of dozens of areas, hundreds of churches, hundreds of cemetery locations, and fourteen crematoria. On top of all this was the internal politics of a haphazard operation where those who managed did not work, and those who worked had to manage.

Very typical situation for Britain as a whole really!

Most of the people who worked there I got on with, after all, the focus from day to day was providing a complaint-free delivery of service to our, mostly grateful, customers. Some of the guys were total bastards, conniving, work-shy and duplicitous. We should always be inspired by bad people and assholes, they are a living example of how we should not to choose to live. They had a personal poverty in their lives that takes a while to understand, and needs a while to know the impact of.

Some advice here, always practice staying in the positive, as positive people will always give more than they know to those around them, and will feed that positivity and the joys that come with it into others lives. Negative people do the total opposite and in letting themselves down, and attempt at all times, either directly or by default, to bring others around them down.

…a natural law of the universe.

In this reality, death is all about life, and vice-versa, and we play the cards in life that nature and the fates have dealt us, learning slowly and surely that it's not necessarily how good a stack of cards one is given in life, although that certainly can help, but how smartly one plays with the cards we are given.

Death is a leveller, an equalizer and a stark reality, and being around it every day as part of my job, it has over the years, changed me for the better as a person.

I suit myself, but not selfishly so, I consider others, but not exccessively so, I reward myself, but not irresponsibly so. It's all about the balance, the yin and the yang thing.

The very reason that I have always respected my personal responsibility for consumption of alcohol is down to contact with families of alcoholics around funerals. Alcoholism wrecks lives, simple as that. Not just the life of the alcoholic but those around them who are courageous enough to remain committed to this ill member of the family, to give them support, probably money, and some of themselves, often too much of themselves, way too much.

Always the innocent suffer.

I will never forget the call that came into the office not long after I had started at the Co-op.

It was a police call, part of a contract with the cities mortuary service to transport deceased people from location of death to the city's mortuary for post-mortem examination. It was the high flats in the Gorbals, a poorer area of the city, has been for generations, a war zone of heroin addiction, boring football, dumb attitudes and poor genetics. The calibre of housing did not help either, but the biggest harm that people did was more often than not, to themselves, by themselves.

Wee Ted the van driver and I headed up in the clanky lift to one of the higher floors where the best views of the city are to be had. Bright sunlight streamed through the dirty reinforced windows illuminating dust and almost cheering up the cultivated squalor of the place, but not quite.

A police woman jumped nervously as we appeared in the corridor and then ushered us into a quiet flat.

Small, basic, unloved, and far less of a home than it used to be.

Outside of the main room she paused "Guys", she said authoritatively, "The father's on his way up soon to see his boy leaving so could you wait for my signal for when he's here?".

"No problem", I responded, understanding immediately the need for the living to acknowledge the transition of the dead, something that matters to people more than we recognise.

Ted and I entered the room, it was dull, silent and detached from the world around it, cheap curtains, cheap carpet, an old-fashioned coffee table, a sagging settee and on the bare wall, above the couch, a cluster of seven photos overlapping and pinned into the plaster with panel pins. A husband, a wife, three young happy children, a beach in England, a summer's day, ice creams, a well-dressed fashionable lady loving being with her family, a man, already sad with the world but smiling through it for his family, at his feet, three empty cans of lager, in his pocket a half bottle of liquor, his hair uncut and uncombed. A reminder of what was then, posted above what was now lying underneath the photos.

Beneath the montage hanging on the wall, the sagging settee bore the frame of a gaunt and lifeless corpse curled foetal into a ball, curled up like a cat, restful and gone. Gaunt and grey his remaining youth all now done in the premature end-game of his life. The bottles of vodka on the table were empty, the cigarette ashtray was full, a chipped saucer with a cup of tea and a plain biscuit remained cold and untouched.

We unfolded our transportation stretcher and carefully lifted the body out of the furniture and onto the stretcher lined with plastic sheeting, and then tied the two restraining straps, one at the top, one at the bottom, thus securing the deceased. Thereafter we placed a dignity cover of heavy duty black vinyl over the stretcher and waited for the policewoman's instruction.

After about ten minutes the squeaking rattle of the lift door could be heard from along the corridor and then the soft rumble of lowered voices in an intensly punctuated conversation happening outside of the flat.

A small and tidy old man entered the room accompanied by the police officer, he paused inside the door as if shivering with the ghosts of many memories over many years.

Now, suddenly seeing us there, he briskly pulled himself back into the *now* and apologised to Ted and myself.

"I'm sorry about this men", he said, "You probably get a lot of this in your job".

We both nodded sympathetically at which point the police woman intervened with her condolences.

"I'm very sorry for your loss sir", she stated.

He shrugged, ignoring her briefly, and looked thoughtfully towards the stretcher now bearing his son.

"Thanks", he responded, he smiled, a weight now seemingly lifted from his thoughts.

"But honestly dear", he continued "That selfish wee fool died to us all long ago and now it's finished we can get on with our lives, I will miss him as he was, after all he was my boy, but not as he became, you can only do what you can, and we never turned our backs on him, not once, even though we should have".

Silence returned, the old man paused in thought then moved back a step and waved us through.

Ted and I lifted the stretcher and left carrying it between us towards the lift, leaving behind the sunlit curtains, leaving the moment, leaving the ghosts, and leaving the survivor with all his memories.

Such is the intensity of an ordinary working day in an extraordinary working job, that out of hours of work, the real world beyond takes on more colours and naunces compared to before.

I drink alone, I drink with friends, little and often, good company, always. Whoever is, or is not there. A few malts and few hours on in the evening, and whilst I rake through the embers of the fire to hot up the flames and coals, I also rake through the embers of my working day and peruse all the constant dramas and happenings as if to refresh the details of that cavalcade of constant human drama. There's always something.

Andy is back on duty as I saunter into Oddbins on the Crowe Road.

The sun is unexpectedly shining again, the encroaching summer air, fresh and warm, all is well with Glasgow and the world.

He is his usual sunny self, a disposition which I admire in people as it generally denotes positivity.

Now here is something important. It's all about positivity and negativity you see, when we are young we don't have the experience of life to make the calibration between positive and negative people and how they impact on our lives, much more so than one might realise.

Take the negative person, they may be occasionally entertaining in their constant negativity of thinking the worst of things, situations, people, others, themselves, and no matter how hard you try to show the positive, they remain dedicated to negativity, and all the worst aspects of peoples lives, they are 'positively' negative, everything is less, people are all worse.

Their company, especially over time just brings you down, and they want that! They win.

Positive people are very different, their company immediately elevates the mood, brings brightness to dullness, people are better thought of, actions are more life-affirming and with their influence, we all grow, develop, and remain more positive. It is never time wasted when in the presence of positive people, they add light to our day and affirm our humanity.

Avoid negative people, don't waste time with them, in the end they always make us less than we should be.

Andy is a positive person, bubbly, bright and energetic, and so is his boss Pete, known in the shop as 'smiley' Pete due to his habit of grinning and being cheerful for most of the time, a cunning disguise for his sharp business sensibility. He looks the part too, wavy long brown hair, an open necked cotton patterned shirt, a comfortable shabby cosmopolitan style with libertine sensibilities, a dedicated disciple of the Greek god Dionysus, god of the grape and harvest, deity of wine and plenty.

I love this place, it feels like a liquor store should be, no airs and graces, no pretentions, no bullshit, just charm, knowledge and good will, and still being about business too.

Andy beckons me to the end of the counter, Pete has just deposited a half-filled bottle with three glasses along with a hastily scribbled note. I shuffle towards the bottle, keeping discreet and not rushing too fast in case some other anonymous customer in the shop should notice, and show too much interest in my free sample!

"It's Clynelish", chirps Andy, "14 years old and at forty six percent though... emmm! definitely chill-filtered and probably with added E150a too", he pauses to let me check-out the bottle label before drams are poured.

"That Brora we had at the tasting a few weeks back sold out pretty quick, thanks to some French guy online who does reviews, seems to know his stuff though, very articulate", he pauses to smell the Clynelish slowly, "This is the next best thing, virtually the same distillery really, right beside each other and sharing warehouses many times over the years".

We both reflect in sober silence on the waxy, fruity complex nature of the malt, "Well it's a bloody sight lot better than that bad malt I got that's not working properly".

Andy rolls his eyes, "Have you not got to the bottom of that yet", he enquires, "Anyway what do you think of this then, a good long finish for the price?"

We both return to the glasses in hand as Pete looks after customers further down the counter, although we try to be discreet they glance up to us now and again as if jealous of my free stuff, Pete soon distracts them with a flyer on forthcoming wine tastings including 'Make your sizzling summer cooler with New Zealand whites'.

I notice it's nearly fully subscribed with enthusiastic wine lovers, or perhaps because it's scheduled for Friday evening it makes a great 'happy hour' for up-market bar crawlers around the west end of the city.

I love the west end of Glasgow, it's so entertainingly pretentious and full of unrealistic, over-entitled people intermixed with university students and eccentrics along with some 'rough rockets' and scallywags. Very eclectic.

Suddenly Andy remembers the scrawled note left by Pete, it's sitting right in front of him, he picks it up and un-scrumples it!

"Did you remember me mentioning that Glasgow had a Whisky Club?" he enquires, "Seems it's not long been on the go and has a few members who really take an interest in whisky".

I'm interested.

"I'm up for it, when and where ?" I ask.

"Well, er!... let me see!" he squints at the paper.

"Two weeks on Sunday, an afternoon time, 2pm, the Pot Still in Hope Street".

Two weeks on Sunday later I made my way up the noisy, diesel smoke polluted hill called Hope Street in the middle of Glasgow city centre and into a small, old fashioned, specialist whisky bar called the Pot Still. It was a lot smaller than I expected. A young barmaid looked up disinterestedly as I entered and even as I let the door go on entering Andy rushed up and grabbed the handle on the outside to join me for the 'meet'.

The bar was quiet save for about a dozen people sitting, spread out on the mezzanine upper-level at the back of the premises. A be-spectecled and bearded grey haired man looking quite portly and well-to-do beckoned us both up to join the group.

"Welcome to Glasgow's Whisky Club where a dram is not a drama", he postulated and after the assembled club members and malt-fans had bunched up to provide two fresh seats our club host and Secretary Bill, who had made us welcome, stood up and indicated to a youngish, tired looking chap who was our 'brand ambassador' for the meet.

"This is Andrew from Jon Mark and Robbo's Whisky and he will be introducing and telling us about the drams today".

Andrew proceeded to give a forgettable commentary about his blended malts in fifty centilitre bottles with 'cheery' labels giving very little information apart from basic tasting references.

First there was the 'fresh fruity one' followed swiftly by the 'rich and spicy one'. There's a pause to proceedings as Andrew the Company rep explains about 'making whisky accessible' and 'taking the mystery out of malts' and 'how single malts are not the only option', then onwards we go into the 'smokey and peaty one', after which further measures are poured for those who want them.

I don't, but Andy does, we are both enjoying ourselves in good company, and Andy is getting cheery, I'm not, the whiskies are decent but the smaller fifty centilitre bottles are off-putting, they represent offering less volume of liquor for the money.

Andrew the brand ambassador is preparing for his final pour, a surprise, something NEW, its the 'smooth and sweeter one' which I can barely taste after the volume of the 'smoky and peaty' version I just finished. Eventually I discover it's fairly bland and forgettable, but that's just me I suppose.

Andrew concludes by pouring a further few drams for those who want them, resulting in several now empty bottles, he sure knows how to impress!

Recently emptied bottles are grabbed by the quickest, as souveniers. The hubbub of conversation thereafter grows in energy and volume and Bill soon restores order with a well timed intimation of the next Club meeting the following month.

A brand ambassador from another whisky Company will be presenting six whiskies to the club and will answer any questions people have. I'm up for it, so's Andy.

A well dressed woman, academic looking, observant and the only female in our group, patiently sitting to my right this afternoon has been reserved, and sober, despite her drams.

She turns to me, "Hello, you're new, arn't you, I'm Juliette, pleased to meet you".

She smiles. I like her immediately.

She's clearly a character.

"Ralfy... whisky dafty!" I reply, she laughs loudly, appreciating my self-effacement.

She leans further towards me lowering her voice to a mumble, "Okay for a warm-up but hardly worth the cost!", she concludes looking first at the bottles, then at the whisky glasses in front of her, then to the presenter, Andrew. "Well, I think they are competent but hardly sparklers, but for the cost and for Sunday afternoon, I'm not complaining". I respond, being ambient in attitude within my creeping, alcohol-haze. Nothing outstanding, but just quite nice... is the way I would sum-up the event.

"The last club evening was Ardbeg, 10 year old, the new Uigeadail cask strength, 1972 and 'Lord of The Isles twenty five year old', now THAT was a Presentation", she affirmed, stabbing the table with her fore-finger to emphasize the point. She returned her upwards gaze back down towards her partially filled whisky glasses sitting neatly in an row, whispering now, she confides "I've had a lot better!", I laugh, she clearly knows her whiskies and her palate.

I pause for a moment, reflecting on Juliette's evident awareness of all things malty.

"I have an off-malt giving me issues and I don't know what the problem is", I suggest.

"Probably the casks, it's usually the casks, most quality-issue problems with any whiskies are to do with the casks being stale, sour, flat, over-used, badly reconditioned, leaking, badly stored, under matured, over matured, partially matured, or sometimes put from one cask to another in the hope it just gets better", she sighs, as if acknowledging her knowing of knowledge.

I'm suitably impressed, it's as if all the small parcels of information, opinion and experience are being brought together in an amplified awareness, an epiphany, a 'eureka' moment!

The afternoon concludes with a hearty round of applause for our weary presenter and an announcement from Bill the Secretary as and where the next Club meeting will be, to everyones satisfaction another brand ambassador and his/her produce are again, intimated.

Everyone there is at the next meeting, it is such good value for money!

As we are heading out the door I am still chatting to Juliette about whisky-stuff and the goods and bads of peated malts when she suddenly remembers to ask something she had not initially intended to mention, "Are you going to the 'Whisky Live' Event in George Square in three weeks ?, there will be drams in tents and tickets don't seem to be selling fast!".

"Reckon I will, anybody else going ?" I ask.

"Just a few of us, some don't think it's a good event with the table staff attitudes and such, but I'm going, there will be an Ardbeg table there".

Back home, the slight euphoric dizziness of the afternoon's sustained malt-moment is still active, fresh and lovely. It's not too much now, which I appreciate.

The kettle is partially filled and goes on the blue-flickering gas, a cheerful steam whistle from the spout denotes the procession to tea-time. The tea is wonderful, so refreshing and I sip slowly as I open up the walk-in cupboard recently cleared of vacuum cleaner, ironing board and spare stuff. On the shelves are now neat rows of bottles, whisky bottles, all labels facing front, all regions separated, all independent bottlings next to official bottlings. There are five hundred bottles, all full, all sealed, all mint condition, all mine, my stash, my precious, precious... I pause, laughing at my absurd association... my Undertakers Stash!

On the Monday I buy a ticket for Glasgow 'Whisky Live'. I'm really looking forward to it.

Chapter Five

Whisky Gigs and Whisky Clubs

Notes.
Slow start, a little disappointing on the palate initially then grows over time towards a much more malt-driven and rounded finale. Worth the effort but a stepping-stone to better things.

Gracious is each new-found day that floods our lives with memories fresh, that feeds our soul with warm accord, and lust for life if we so choose, whilst seeking love, perchance to love life more. We embrace ourselves for we are gold, we are charmed and we are star-dust if we so choose to be. Blessed is the arrival of our new day and with sleep's concluding breeze we arise and stretch towards the light, breathing deeply, for we surely must and let our lives be more, so much more, more than they were the day before.

I bought a ticket for my first ever 'Whisky Live' in Glasgow. Got dressed up smart and neat for the special occasion and went to the Smiddy down at the end of my road for a pre-event pint of Youngers No3.

It's Saturday morning, and a cool summer wind drifts politely along Dumbarton Road, and past the opened door of the Smiddy. It's been jammed open with some rolled up newspaper, still wet from the dirty mop used to redistribute the grime off shoe soles and stuff dropped.

The air inside is thick with stale cigarette smoke and stale beer, something in the smell of the place that I have got to know over the years is missing, and I don't know what it is.

I know what it isn't, it's not the cloying, sweet reek of concentrated air 'freshener' which has been over-used in too small a space, my eyes start to nip.

"Whaat 'ye 'wannt?" whines a voice from behind the bar.

I immediately spot badly washed glasses stacked indiscriminately across the back shelves, they clearly don't belong there.

The voice cuts into my contemplation again, louder this time, more aggressive, "Ye got an order then?" barks a petite and over-dressed young woman from the corner of the bar, just behind the till where she is reading receipts fresh-churned from the cash register. She does not look up.

"Pint of No3... please".

"That 'wans no in stock now, d'ye want a guinness instead?".

I don't.

I leave.

I don't look back.

I never return to the Smiddy.

I am now publess, this bar a stranger to me now. It hurts.

As I walk down the road towards the subway station at Kelvin-hall, I'm still stinging from the shock of such a familiar venue which has been so much a part of my whisky-journey, suddenly morphing into an unwelcoming place, that I get all nostalgic for the times when James was behind the bar mastering the ship, and Sanny the cooper was in front of it, drinking to quell the storms within his days. These precious moments are gone, completely, and I appreciate the nature of nostalgia a little bit more now. I console myself with the mission to find a new bar.

First there is a Whisky Festival to attend, I take the rattling subway train into the city centre, known locally as the 'clockwork orange' due to it's brightly painted orange carriages and regularity of availability. There is always a fascinating smell to the subway, a sort of musty, mould smell of the sort one finds around obscure matured cheeses of good quality.

These days I notice I smell more, and also in more detail, more of everything.

In George Square, a series of large off-white marquees have been erected side by side and end to end to offer a large conference space for events. Todays event is 'Glasgow Whisky Live' promoted with little publicity, or information, except for the availability of 'superb' whiskies from Scotland for the discerning connoisseur. I hand over my ticket to a very polite lady at reception who hands me a leaflet, booklet containing a floor plan of the presenters, a whisky glass, and a small cheap-looking tab of ten 'tokens' to swap for samples of whisky.

I wander around the venue to get my bearings before attempting any offerings from the unimaginatively decorated tables scattered like a wagon train around the edges, leaving large spaces between them interupted occasionally with up-ended barrels. Despite having commenced an hour previously, the event does not seem to have sold many tickets.

It's not exactly what you would call busy.

I soon find out why.

Steeling myself for the initial dram I walk up to a table presented in a plain white table cloth, a plate of oatcakes, a jug of water and five near-full bottles of malt whisky, all different ages and all from the same distillery.

"Could I have a wee drop of the twenty year old?", I ask.

"Sure", says the young lady in the tartan dress with tartan bow. "That will be three coupons please!"

I pause, confused, "But I was told at the entrance that it's one coupon per dram".

"Yeeees", she replies, politely but unsympathetically, "but that's for the younger malts but older ones need more coupons. You can have the ten year old for one coupon, oh, and you can always buy more coupons when you run out!"

Now I think I know why tickets are not selling.

I request the twenty year old for three coupons, now I am down to seven coupons and I WON'T be buying anymore from this table.

My thoughts turn a little negative as I contemplate the cynics who are responsible for organizing the event in conjunction with an ongoing lack of demand for whisky in the wider world.

Surely this sort of event should be a showcase, a positive ambassador, an opportunity to 'taste and try before you buy'.

Someone out there in the Industry never got the memo, or never cared to read it, possibly they just don't have to care at all.

It's still a quiet and increasingly soulless gig as I wander round enjoying my twenty year old malt, whilst in my head I contemplate how to 'spend' the other seven tokens.

There's a Whyte and MacKay installation down in the bottom area, and I wander down to see what the flurry of activity is which is now generating a little life into the place. The ever immaculate, and animated, master blender Richard Paterson from Whyte and Mackay Distillers is hosting a wedding.

Already in my limited journey through malts I consider that this Company's offerings are over-priced and over-caramelised and over-filtered.

They can be good, often they are good whisky bottled bad.

Richard is in good form today, already the floor is reeking of spilled and splashed whiskies cast down in an act of thespian flourish which is something Richard is good at doing. Oscar Wilde would be entertained.

Richard has the duty of priest, filling his role admirably, and he is 'marrying' two clearly embarrassed looking young helpers in 'wedded bliss'... sort-of.

They are both now holding hands and trying not to squirm at the complete hamminess of the malt-infused pantomime.

"Aaaand Naaow", bellows Richard, "Weee briiing togggethurr, sherry and bourbon in holy matrimonnyyyy", he ad-libs, "Forever toggg-etherrr, forever", he quips, "In a cask fusion of perfecshunnn!"

"Sherry, you may kiss bourbon", he proclaims with a flourish.

Sherry pretends to kiss bourbon, and succeeds.

Some people watching cheer, but I think they are staff, a few more clap some polite applause, most look on bemused by the spectacle. As soon as the ceremony concludes, the newly-weds head off in opposite directions to avoid further embarrassment. I spend one coupon on a sample of Jura ten year old.

I don't finish it. I pour what I don't drink on the same patch that Richard poured his drams. It's a big wet patch.

Such a shame, as Jura, the Distillery produces an excellent signature of a malt, nutty, malty and characterful, but best bought from Independent bottles who don't cosmetify it with colourant and chill-filtering.

In truth, Richard Patterson is an excellent and inspired master blender, truly talented for the role, and he has given a lot of identity to Whyte and Mackay over the years which their style of commerce is hardly worthy of... in my opinion!

Of all the thousands of bottles of whisky I have bought over the decades from many producers, the fewest have been from this Company, my own, and other malt-mates experiences have created this situation.

I strongly suspect it's a leadership thing.

They are lucky to have Richard.

He will be very hard to replace when he's gone.

I do wish his successor all the best, it will be a hard gig.

I wander off to the next table, an independent bottler with the 'ambassador' showing some interest in his task. I ask for some twenty-six year old malt from a less-known distillery now closed and beyond production. He acknowledges my care and respect for the dram, and as I offer three coupons in payment, he smiles sympathetically as accepts just one coupon and discreetly returns two others back to me. He winks.

I make a mental note to buy several bottles from this producer on my next shopping trip.

We chat... amicable, friendly, he is knowledgable, clearly so, and happy to give me the time.

It's not exactly busy anyway.

The malt is delicious, ethereal, complex, clean and bright thanks to being bottled at cask strength, with natural colour and unchillfiltered.

I take my time with this one, he then offers me another, a different closed distillery I have not heard of before, North Port, it is equally as delicious as the previous dram.

At last, I am now warming to the experience of my first whisky festival.

The next table shatters that mellowed mood.

Ardbeg really thinks it's something special, the stand is situated as an island near the centre of the marquee. Sober, minimalist and all dark green stuff.

The attitude of the hired model brought in to pour the measures is impatient and disinterested, and she's similar to the two others next to her on the stand.

I ask for a dram of the ten year old version. She asks for my ticket before she will pour.

It's good, tasty, peaty and Ardbeg-y.

The model in front of me folds her arms in defence mode and stares into the middle distance, so no conversation here then!

I offer a compliment to warm the chill, "You look amazing, that dress really suits you so well", I lie.

This flattery suddenly transforms her into a giggly willow.

She seems to be loving the attention, I seem to be filling a void in her day now.

"Like this malt, you clearly have good taste" I add.

Now she's gushing in enthusiasm for me, it's getting a bit too much, too soon.

Suddenly she stoops under the table and draws out a new bottle of Ardbeg, 'Uigeadail' it says on the label.

Fluttering her eyes she pours me a large measure and takes my offered ticket.

It's stunningly good; a good malt, carefully crafted, excellent active casks delivering a fresh intense signature of this deservedly noteworthy brand.

I thank her sweetly, and move away from the table almost bumping into Juliette who has appeared beside me with her friend.

"What's that you got there", she chirps.

"Ardbeg Uigeadail", I respond.

"From under the table, it's new and a special version".

"Indeed", Juliette replies, "So special that only men seem to be getting a dram if they offer enough flattery to the hosts". I pause, look for a minute... and see that she's right enough.

There's an awkward silence, broken by Juliette who has mischief on her mind.

"Could you take my empty glass up and get them to fill it with the Uigeadail?" she requests.

Two patient and faked minutes later I return with virtually a double measure of the whisky for Juliette. She takes the glass, raises it in silent toast to the models behind the table who now know what has happened and are furious.

Juliette, her friend and I walk off, we won, they lost, job done. They're just not happy... we are.

"Quiet, isn't it", quips Juliette's pal, a slim and articulate man who's name I never get to remember.

He rhymes off the whiskies he's tried, and is now leaving as he has had enough of the atmosphere.

Juliette and I continue to talk about whisky-stuff as we stroll around the event on another clock-wise lap when she notices the entrance busying up, it seems that towards the last hour of the show, due to poor ticket sales, all remaining tickets are now being sold half-price with what appears to be three rounds of coupons. A raggle-taggle of middle class, middle aged men fresh from local bars march purposefully to the nearest table and demand doubles of whatever, Juliette and I are quite non-plussed, a little bemused and totally unimpressed. We decide to leave early as there is an increasingly agitated *tone* to the Show.

The Glasgow's Whisky Club meets again, it is fun, informal and also a great source of both good whiskies and good company. There are about twenty members, although I would have thought there would be more than that, due to the exceptional value that the Club provides in sourcing great whiskies at relatively low cost to members for tasting.

I suppose that meeting on a Tuesday night near the city centre deters the more hard-core weekend drinker conditioned to detoxing during week days. Our monthly meetings take on a growing depth and character as brand ambassadors continue to show an interest in presenting their range of products for consideration and comparison by us increasingly knowledgable 'anoraks'.

I would like to say it was out of the goodness of their hearts, but this is not the case, within the club are journalists, Industry professionals, some very good 'noses' for articulating whiskies, and people increasingly using social media such as Facebook and Google to talk and blog about all things whisky. Many distilleries have picked up on this and see the best way to connect with these changes and opportunities is by offering to present their brands informally and with willingness to listen to any compliments and criticisms. It's a strategy which seems to work for them, and the Club.

We contribute to food and beverage columns in a local newspaper, we tweet, we blog, we engage with the brand reps beyond the usual level of superficiality.

Most of all, we drink responsibly and there are never any 'uncomfortable' moments associated with members drinking habits in these early days.

During these club years a number of stunningly good whiskies were discovered and much was learned from well-informed people. I remember a sample of Scotch Malt Whisky Societies No13 bottling of Glenmorange, a thirteen year, single cask, cask strength version of incredible character and quality, simply an unforgettable malt, also, a twenty-one year old Carsebridge single grain whisky from an Independent bottler which was the finest column still grain scotch I have ever tasted. I went out the following day and bought two bottles, easy to do as then the price was less than half of what single malts were selling for. People did not rate or value scotch grain column still whisky then, they were considered 'lesser' beings.

Jarkko the athletic bohemian Finnish ballet dancer is always good for a laugh, a later member of the Club he brought a touch of the libertine into the group which lent a cosmopolitanised, urbane air to Club nights.

Generally, unless a brand ambassador rep was presenting their offerings, there would be about twenty opened bottles sitting on an up-ended cask and we would just help ourselves. After a 'few', Jarkko would regale us with stories of his military training in

Finland where conscription is still in force and describe how to break someone's neck on the battlefield followed by the rigours of ongoing dance training as one of the Royal Scottish Ballet Corps dancers. I popped in a few undertaker related tales of family feuds, drunken clergy and mishaps with carrying coffins.

Another character by the name of Bobby Banford is a quietly greying, unassuming intellect, with an insightful take on reality, who deconstructs malts in his glass with almost surgical precision, whilst casting our way well aimed insults and 'funnies'.

Halcyon days!

It is not long before the Club moves out of the Pot Still in Hope Street to look for a bigger venue to accommodate growing Club membership. On our last meet at the Pot Still I asked the barman if I could take a few pictures of the bottles along the gantry for an online blog I was planning to create.

My request was not well received.

"NO", he said bluntly, "No pictures allowed".

I didn't argue, I said 'thanks' and left him to scowl at his gantry. He must have been having a bad day, on leaving I noticed the gantry was not holding as many illustrious bottles as it used to.

After a few uncomfortable venue options were trailed and found wanting for various reasons, some reasons being practical, some reasons being remoteness from public transport, we discovered ourselves in a larger established whisky bar where the reception and atmosphere was a lot more convivial. It sent a shiver down my spine of nostalgia and childhood memories as I attended my first club night at the Bon Accord in North Street, Charing Cross.

Many years before, my father, who worked at the Mitchell Library next door to the Bon Accord bar, would make the most of a 1970s'-era train strike to phone my mother up and instruct her to drive into Glasgow and collect him from the old bar next to the Library.

It is traditional in style, a long, dark, shiny oak bar with wall mirrors, lots of imposing beer pumps, and clouds of thick glutinous threads of high-tar cigarette smoke drifting around the air, looking for escape into the outside chill as soon as the door opens to admit or exit another patron. In the nineteen seventies, when real ale was in its infancy, the Bon Accord was a beacon of wholesome flavours, and quality traditional ales. One evening after much delay due to heavy road traffic as a result of yet another rail strike, my mother and I arrived outside the bar and as she did not want to go into a 'man's place' I was nominated as a teenager... just a young boy really, to go in and fetch out my father before he bought yet another pint.

It was a bit exciting, after all bars were for grown-up's and this was my first ever foray into such a place, I had absolutely no idea what to expect.

I push open the heavy, solid door which responds with a brassy squeak from the worn hinges, and immediately a wraith of yellow-ish cigarette smoke billows out into the fresher cold night air. The bar looks bright, huge and magnificent, and a few local worthies are propped up on tall slender bar stools looking round in curiosity as a youngster peeks nervously into the premises.

I can not see him at all, I enter a little more, further into the drinkers paradise, further into the *den*, there was still no sign of that familiar face until after about a twenty seconds, a voice catches my attention from an alcove tucked just out of sight on the right hand side, "Be with you in a minute", he calls, swilling down the last few dregs of another much enjoyed glass of hoppy goodness. We leave, go home, life returns to normal, days then years go by and after all this time I have once again ventured into the Bon Accord, this time as an adult, and enjoying liquor just as much as my father did, probably more so!

Even as I approached the green solid door, obviously the same one from thirty years previously, I shuddered at the familiar squeak of the same brass hinges as I slowly swung the door open to enter, the same bar, the same wooden floor boards, the same down-lit ex-tensive gantry which was now far more opulently stocked with a tremendous variety of whisky bottles, more than I have seen in any other bar, ever. It was now smoke-free due to the changes in law and attitude over the years and now the lighting seemed more in-tense, focused, directed at beer pumps and bottles. The gantry shimmered like an Aladdin's cave of malted treasures, and several cheerfully busy staff shimmied up and down pouring pints and measuring out portions of liquor from metal measure-cups into glencairn glasses, a style of tough nosing glass designed for, and adopted across the scotch whisky scene.

It was busy, the rumble of animated conversation ebbing and flowing according to the flickering activity of a football match playing out on a large monitor firmly anchored by sturdy steel brackets to the remaining free space above the front doorway. Despite the activity I could not initially see any sign of the familiar sociable faces of whisky club-members, my enquiring gaze continued to scan for a few more seconds, ignoring the bar, looking at people.

A tall, white-haired, slightly red-faced man sitting on a bar stool within viewing range of the front door noticed my situation immediately, suggesting a passively-active awareness of all that was happening around him, he beckoned me across with a friendly wave, "You meeting someone mate?" he asked, "Er, um, there's a whisky club meeting here tonight and I think I might be the first to arrive!" he chuckled, "No yer no, there's six through the back having a dinner, are you looking for something to eat before it starts?" I declined the offer and made off through to the seating area beyond the back of the bar which I had failed to notice when I first arrived.

"By the way", he called after me, "I will join you's later for a dram, I'm Paul by the way, I run the place... it's my bar", I nod and return an acknowledging wave, continuing down some steps into what was clearly a well patronised dining section with the smell of food wafting towards me over the chatter of brisk conversations, and smelling good too, making me hungry again after my hurried half-cooked dinner at home only an hour previously, rushed as always, in case I might be late and miss a malt-moment!

Bill, the Club secretary was holding court at a large table with five other malt-clubbers busy eating and listening intently. Bill was clearly making plans for us as a group and access to good whisky was the subject. He stood up and waved me across "Saved you a seat Ralfy", he chuckled, "Rock-up and sit down, we could use your articulate nose tonight".

After the finished plates had been removed and replaced with fresh pints of ale and whisky glasses, Bill introduced the night's schedule for us all to review, discuss, and comment on the bottles he had been given by distillers and to give opinion on, and to give feedback to, the producers.

It was a quieter than usual club night and I got the impression that Bill had organised a hand-picked team of club regulars to focus on a Newspaper article he was planning which would provide useful publicity to the drams we were about to short-list for inclusion.

Simultaneously, he was checking out the Bon Accord as a new club venue option prior to a conventional club meeting and tasting session. We all agreed that the atmosphere was positive, the ambiance definitively whisky-ish and the space, if we could monopolise the mezzanine section of the dining area, was good for up to thirty people.

Bill continued, "Agreed then team that we will now limit our club membership to thirty people at a time, I'm getting some growing interest out there about the club, people seem to be showing more of an interest in whisky these days!"

We all agree and set ourselves to dismantling the samples in glasses before us.

It's fun, a lot of fun, good company, good venue, good craick, some good drams, but not all, just some, a few bottles on the table are offering flat, mediocre, lack-lustre experiences and as a team we nosed, sipped, nosed and tasted systematically to narrow down the issues of good, and bad, and why it was so. Shared opinion is invaluable to learning about spirits in all their convoluted guises.

I learned an incredible amount from the people around me in Glasgow's Whisky Club during those early days of malted discoveries.

No wonder... they included Industry professionals who could articulate how flavours were created in different regions from different-shaped stills in different altitudes and my awareness of the impact of casks both in flavour-influence, and form-effect on whiskies was astounding when examined more closely than was feasible before, due to inexperience coupled with lack of awareness.

All this shared experience was there around the table, Jarkko provided his laconic Finnish humour and mock-snobbery, Bobby Banford articulated the subtle notes of smell and taste in each of the glasses with his amazing perception, and Juliette kept us grounded and focussed on our mission in maltiness to ensure that the night did not go on too long for safety!

Bill over-viewed proceedings from the top of the table occasionally taking notes, and doing his cheer-meister to maintain our engagement with the nights's mission. At the end of the evening some decent and comprehensive notes are taken and a newspaper article was in its first draft.

I'm not sure what I provided, but they seemed to like me, and I to like them, so all was well. I offer a few additional words here and there and they seemed to be added to the growing script for printing.

As the evening wore on, Paul arrived from his pilot's seat at the end of the bar and joined us in avoiding the lesser whiskies in favour of the better whiskies, his comments and perspectives adding further to the quality of our press-release.

An interestingly odd Glengoyne seventeen year old malt got a frown or two, it was off-key, flat and savoury in a bad way, a diminishing way, which seemed to be a sum total of less character, flavour quality and nose articulance.

We all discussed it for some time and it was observed that batch quality variation was variable between distilleries, some like Glenfiddich, Ancnoc and Glenmorangie were reliably consistent from year to year, others were not so consistent.

The evening concluded with an invite to Paul the proprietor to join the Glasgow's Whisky Club which he graciously accepted and we finished up at the time that Bill's wife the 'fragrant Babbette' appeared waiting patiently to drive him home.

I finished my drams, I finished my pint of casked ale, I finished my whisky-chats and malt-gossiping and headed out into the cold, wet night air where the chill of the restless wind blowing some litter along the pavement did nothing to lessen the residual warmth inside of me from the alchemic convergence of sun-ripened barley grains, ethanol and the further enhancement of good company in a solid environment with echos of sincere opinion and good cheer.

After a refreshingly long walk, to sober up a bit, I arrived back home to the glowing embers of a fading fire in the hearth, to which I added a few more coals, but not too many, as I would be heading off to bed within the hour. The fire crackled and sparked alive again and it seemed such a shame to waste the fresh glowing warmth emanating from the flickering flames, that I reach into the cabinet and pull out a bottle to pour one small, final night-cap before sleep finds me dozing still half awake, to wrap me in slumber's soft and dreamless oblivion.

I notice another bottle unopened, Glengoyne seventeen years old, still sealed.

Would it be the same, or different from the awkward sample experienced earlier that evening ?

I pondered for a minute, there is only one way to find out, I rip the seal, pop the cork and pour a wee dram, it's different, very different, so, so much cleaner, expressive and articulate of what this great wee distillery can do with it's unpeated, toffied malt.

This was bliss, pure bliss, I could not rush it, that would be a sin, a crime, a negligence, an abuse.

Quickly I went through to my bedroom and pulled off a pillow and the duvet from the bed, dragging them through to my front room where the fire was now in full flame-dancing mood and I curled up on the carpet in front of the fire, siping my malt and savouring my malt, slowly and with care, allowing my thoughts to be caught up on the gentle breezes of possible dreamscapes entwined with improbable realities, circling in blissful silence and a cozy, flame-lit darkened room, where fresh shadows now play and dance across my ceiling and walls, shielding off the outside world in all it's madding maelstrom of life and death and joy and sorrow and everything.

I am alone and in perfect companionship, resting in a place that angels might choose to rest for company, and for their share more freely offered than in a cold and draughty warehouse somewhere on a wind-swept hillsides, damp and dull.

I see them in the shadows as I lay ensconced, deep within my padded blanket, with head half resting on a now folded pillow. Let these angels have their share and company.

Now some forgiven devils join us too, observant, mute and wise, rewarded for redeemed transgressions, and risen high above their circumstance to belong now to a discovered enchanted moment, fleeting but endless, within the confines of a little home where the amber of divine spirit caresses the fogging head of a sleep-kissed mortal who, for just a moment, a brief but endlessly short moment, dances with these angels and devils, and in a place far from heaven and hell.

Another place, a separate place, golden place where sleep creeps across the nights unending sentinel and keeps me company till the dawning of a new and freshened day.

Chapter Six

Cask Culture and Malt-Moments

Notes.
Soft start and typical lowland characteristics weave into a fruity and sweet development worth the wait.

It was a good idea at the time. Get totally into whisky for the varieties, the adventures, the company, the banter, the community, the smells, the flavours, the.... soft intoxication at the end of the day, to usher in deeper, untroubled sleep.

Thanks to a sudden and unexpected education from a seventeen year old malt from Glengoyne I finally understood what was happening with my now sadly abandoned old bottle of disappointing malt.

Casks, it really is all about the casks. To know casks is to know whisky. I had been told, but needed to discover this properly for myself.

And casks are about wood, oak wood primarily.

World wide there are roughly about two thousand species of oak, of which about thirty are structurally suitable, and economical for utilisation as casks, being sourced, felled, transported, rested, milled, rested, seasoned, cut, shaped, softened, bent, shaped again, assembled, coopered, tested, toasted or charred, or both, rested, filled, plugged, stored, months, years, decades, emptied, reconditioned, reused, eventually discarded, for furniture, for ornaments, for wall hangings, for bar features, for burning, for smoking, for heat, for gardens, for land-fill.

There are a lot of casks around the world, and lots of them are in Scotland, some that have existed for a hundred years or more, their job being to hold, store, mature, season, oxidise, mellow, complify and help whisky simply survive for as long as possible, until needed for profit, commerce, entertainment, bribe, gift, present, apology, reward, self-indulgence, intoxication, sublime smells, divine flavours, rough rot-gut, cleaner, collections, investment, speculation, divination, ritual, sharing, detachment, bliss, and quite a lot of other things too.

Oak is not the only wood in the forest, for the purposes of cask construction, cherry and chestnut are also used with great success in America and throughout Europe, and it's now not unusual to hear of exotic woods like amburana from Brazil being used as flavouring staves, chips, wood dust, inner cask staves, all for adding further flavours to spirits.

Humanoids don't eat wood, it's too chewy, indigestible, unpleasant, sometimes toxic, however it is well recorded that plants make for great flavours and good examples are cinnamon, which is a powdered tree bark, and quinine, also extracted from tree bark. Sugars can be obtained from trees such as maple syrup and birch juice. Shrub berries make coffee, shrub leaves make tea.

There is more variety and intensity of smell and flavour to be found in the plant world compared to any other source, even modern refined coal extracts from chemical laboratories.

I love smell and taste, the smell of orchids are examplified by the stanophea, a powerfully scented hanging tree orchid which uses perfume to intoxicate pollinating insects, and make them stay in the flower longer. The perfume of the stanophea is more complex than any cosmetic perfume I have ever encountered. Night scented stock, small pink flowers which grow on spindly stems up to two feet high are enchanting and unlike any other smell you will ever encounter, night stock is the smell of seductive enchantment by the natural world, a glimpse for mortals into the unfathomable, supernatural beyond the mortal blindfold!

Because we don't really smell wood much, unless we are in a joiners workshop or timber mill, we tend to view wood as of neutral character, without smell, without taste.

It's how we are conditioned in society to view things, wood is for soft forest smells as we walk through a wooded area when out for a stroll, wood is for functional furniture, window frames, seats, tables, benches, all devoid of smell, and all unlikely to be tasted.

The flavour of wood is best appreciated when immersed in solvent in the form of potable ethanol, also recognised as smelling and drinking alcohol. The ethanol slowly impregnates some of the wood, dissolving the natural flavourant chemicals in the form of esters, phenols and acetones amongst other stuffs.

Over time, the smell and flavours adjust, re-compose, refine and layer in a graduation from simpler objective composites like lemon, vanilla and barley sugar to more obscure and subjective composites like leather, tobacco and mustiness. The range and sequence of flavours are extensive and complex, further amplified by the morphing over time in casks of the sensations of sweet, sour, bitter, salt and savoury. They commence as simple components. From new they make the spirit morph, over time, into far more ethereal, complex and ultimately rewarding inclusions in a cask-aged whisky. Some whiskies are simply better younger, like Glenfiddich, others work better older, like Glen Grant, most are more chameleon and versatile working very well whatever the cask and how ever long matured, like Bruichladdich, Springbank and Clynelish.

Some malts like Glenfarclas, Aberlour and Glen Elgin appear to suit their maturation in ex-sherry casks where more spice and savoury notes evolve with the spirits whilst others seem better suited to ex-bourbon casks like Auchentoshan, Benrinnes and Old Pulteney.

The observation of cask-culture is the one aspect of matured spirits production, whether whisky, rum, brandy or bourbon that will always throw up new insight and illumination as time goes on. Sure, the still shape, format, layout and size matters, the yeast, the grain, grape or sugar source, the cultivation and crafting of product to the *location* and *provenance* of a distillery, but history lessons and statistics will not let one be familiar and acquainted with base new-make spirits... how they change, mature, evolve or remain relatively unchanged over time. Only in casks and with time is where there is always something new 'found' and accidentally created by mother nature that may surprise, entertain, astonish, confuse and illuminate the imbiber.. Only methodical tasting and smelling can do a well crafted whisky justice.

That is the unique provenance of cask-culture, and always noticed more in traditional dunnage warehouses, also known as lodges.

It takes time to recognise how location of cask storage affects the eventual product. It's not just the warehouse's fluctuating ambient temperature, casks heights off the ground, scale of racking and cask containment volume, plus other assorted cask-influencing elements to storage, the *feel* of a place will impact too, especially if you visit the warehouse then tasting the spirit, there's a 'connect' and it's significant, more significant than many people realise.

Can I give you some practical Scottish advice, especially if you are a motorcyclist.

When the British annual bank holiday weekends arrive during the unravelling of the year and given the situation that as a result of supposed State generosity working people get an extra day off added to their weekend; - so a Saturday and Sunday end up a Saturday, Sunday, Monday, precious time!

Many head to traditional parts of the nation considered more beautiful, more desirable and in keeping with social norms, the few narrow and precipitous roads that lead from central Scotland up to the highlands get grid-locked, not just congested, but rammed with traffic and increasingly aggressive vehicle drivers. Also, at some point, the rain will arrive with a cold, wet, miserable efficiency practiced over millions of years.

Then some biker will crash and get killed, it always happens!

I never head north from Glasgow, I get on my trusty Triumph Thunderbird Sport motorcycle and head south. Not south to England, although the Lake District is charming and never boring, but south-west to the southern coast of Scotland where it meets the Irish Sea.

The Dumfries and Galloway region of Scotland is often totally over-looked by visitors and natives too who will head no further south than the pretty and sea-sidy town of Largs for a paddle, ice cream and much needed chill out.

I go further, much further, down to Port Patrick, Logan Botanic, Creetown, and Newton Stewart.

It's always drier, warmer, less crowded, more amicable, softer in nature and cleaner in environment.

The Mull o' Galloway is my favourite spot... it's a sea and sky thing with me!

And there is also a distillery, a wee, old fashioned, charming and friendly distillery called Bladnoch.

When looking at remote distilleries around Scotland it tends to be Talisker, Mull, Highland Park and Old Pulteney which get the recognition, however in terms of actual *feel* of remoteness, for me, Bladnoch tops the list.

On my first visit, many years ago now, I was ambling south-east along the B7005 road on the motorbike when suddenly there appeared a sturdy, stone arched bridge over the river Bladnoch, then over on the left an instantly recognisable silhouette of distillery roofs, complete with iconic Doig cupola pagoda chimney cover. scattered, squat, traditional, stone, cosy and characterful.

The location is perfect, a small roundabout divides the bridge with its telephone kiosk, the distillery itself, an old whitewashed public house and finally a meander of straggling hedges bordering the river.

I parked up, wandered in and quickly found the visitors centre which was primarily a shop with a wide range of single cask and small batch bottlings at higher strength, no marketing 'theme', no cliched music, no video screen with rasping sound track, just a confidently old-fashioned green-painted, wood decorated shop featuring bottles of Bladnoch whisky and a few practical and carefully chosen accessories like hats and scarves.

A bright-eyed and immediately friendly little dark-haired lady busied herself behind a high-topped wooden counter, "Be with you in a wee minute", she chirped!

Bright sunlight now suddenly glanced throughout the shop widows as a cottonwool cloud departed onwards overhead, allowing the intense sunlight to sparkle again, glancing golden light through the glass of the whisky bottles neatly lined up across the windows, now I could smell the tang of whisky, mellow, aromatic, soft, grainy and butterscotch.

I felt the love.

"Now, what can I do for you sweetheart?" the wee lady asked, half laughing.

"Err umm, I would like to buy a bottle of whisky".

She laughed again, "Well you're in the right place, and have you got time for a wee dram?"

She poured from a recently opened bottle sitting amongst others on a tray placed, strategically, on a small bar in a side room, fifteen year old Bladnoch bottled at 55% vol:, the liquor splashed around the inside of the glencairn and settled thereafter into a syrupy looking haze of amber glow. I thanked her, "ooch, no worries m'dear... I'm Yolanda, by the way, you enjoy the wee dram and if you need any help selecting a bottle just give me a shout!"

"I'm Ralfy, a whisky geek", I replied.

Fresh voices drifted up from the front door and Yolande scuttled off to attend to the new visitors leaving me alone in the silence and calm of the place.

I picked up the bottle, it was a standard layout but featured an unusual label design.

The glossy green label had sheep on it, two in fact, a mum and her lamb.

Bladnoch
Aged 15 Years
Single Lowland Malt
(An oval picture of two sheep)
Black Faced Sheep, artist – Jan Ferguson
The most southerly distillery in Scotland
Established 1817
70cl – 55%vol:

A small card tag around the neck of the bottle showed it to be sherry cask matured.

It was delicious, totally in keeping with the lowland style of single malts.

Hesitant in arrival on the nose, soft, understated, shy, the taste revealed a bold fresh sherry cask fruitiness, the dried fruit variety of raisin, sultana and a little fig. Harsh and ethanolic at first it soon mellowed and complexified steadily after the addition of a few large drops of water which were found in a 'bladnoch' ceramic jug at the end of the bar top.

Bladnoch is a definitive lowland malt style and character.

Over the years I have grown to applaud this often overlooked and underrated region of Scotch whisky. The Lowlands region arguably includes Springbank, Glen Scotia and Glengoyne and are more recognised as Auchentoshan, Glenkinchie, Daftmill, Annandale, Littlemill, Rosebank, Linlithgow (St Magdelene) and Bladnoch.

Older official bottlings from all these distilleries are often excellent complex and communicative drams which often reward patience and the subliminal pursuit of refined detail in the development and finish of taste.

Sure, some lowland malts can be awful, delivering short on smell and taste, however this is more often down to lazy production including : -

- cheaper sourced barley,
- hasty fermentation,
- too fast, or over-distillation,
- under-active and stale casks,
- bottling at 40%vol:
- chill-filtration,
- adding E150a colourant,

All these things kill the calibre of smell and taste that scotch lowland malts can achieve.

Even to this day is pisses me off big time that there are some professionals in the whisky industry who wilfully down grade production standards of spirits because they pander to 'the category', and wish to replace intrinsic quality of production with over-monied marketing policies which seek to distract customers from the real-deal!

Lazy investment, to promote a lazy market, of lazy consumers, and all to save money from where it's actually needed, in order to spend money where it has no need to be spent, generating fiction and illusion and sometimes, disingenuous bullshit. Why?

There's no need for it except to reward non producing employees at the expense of those who do matter to the business and who do produce.

I turn my attention back to the glass in my hand, the amber juice is softening further and transmitting more of what it was, is and will be, from assertive to suggested, from intense to immense, from promising to inspiring, from glass to my tummy.

It's looking good and I am inspired and alive within the moment.

On finishing the glass, I wipe my mouth with my sleeve, and for just a minute consider sweet-talking another glass of something similar from out of Yolanda's obvious generosity, however I have priorities including a wander round and peek into the nooks and crannies of the place.

I nod thanks to my hostess as I head outside again promising as I go, that I will be back in when I leave, to buy a bottle or two of whatever she recommends.

Outside the air is fresh, cool, almost cold for the time of year, and even the passing sparkles of sunshine bouncing off the brown stone walls huddling around me cannot prevent a shiver or two.

I pause, deciding which direction to go in when a door opens then closes with a clatter, initially I don't see the direction of the noise as it is coming from up at the top of a flight of metal stairs just to my right hand side. A small, wiry, grey haired man is bouncing athletically down the steps holding an empty coffee mug and clearly looking for a refill.

"Hello there, fine day", he says as he passes briskly by, cheerily nodding a nonchalant greeting as one does when addressing strangers for the first time in a positive manner.

He walks on by leaving me to the atmosphere and presence of the distillery itself, small, elegant, industrial, nostalgic, with brown weathered stone walls at every angle around me, low and intimate.

I like this place more. I feel its presence deeply.

I wander across to the far side of the small courtyard in which I am standing as I can hear the murmur of several voices inside a doorway, with periodic clinking of bottles animating conversation. Entering a poorly lit, but open space surrounded by whitewashed walls and history, I come across a small hands-on bottling plant spread out too far for ergonomic sense but making full use of the ample space available. A young, tousle-headed man and dapper young lady are busy hand-bottling and label-sticking at a trestle table, whilst across the room two gnarly work-worn older men, one small and lean, the other large and rotund, are syphoning out of a sherry hogshead barrel into a stainless steel drum secured inside a metal cage on wheels. They nod some recognition to my sudden presence and then carry on as they were, emptying casks and bottling liquor.

Old-fashioned, labour intensive, rustic and traditional, and very satisfying to watch. The younger tousle-headed chap at the table finishes filling another bottle and stops for a minute to allow his female helper to catch up with the labelling, this is slow as she is being exact and methodical in the precise positioning of each singular but identical label ensuring it is positioned at just the right height thanks to the reference provided by a bottle-holding dolly cradle laying at a forty five degree angle and allowing the extra precision of label placement to happen. She seems a 'precise' person, carefully dressed in cheap clothes including thrift-shop accessories which seem to work well for her. She looks smart and alert and is clearly loving her job. Tousle head casts a cheeky grin across the room towards me, "You here for the tour then?" he enquires with interest, "Starts in twenty minutes and I will be showing everybody round", there's a pause, "I'm Martin by the way, have you tried our whisky yet?" I affirm that I have, and not only that, I have totally enjoyed the dram Yolande poured for me, then, being a total whisky-anorak, I forensically deconstruct why I enjoyed the whisky so much and how I appreciate natural coloured, higher strength, unchill-filtered and *honest* malts.

This monolog lasting a few brief minutes seems to go down very well with the Team, "and!" I conclude, "... am in Glasgow's Whisky Club on the tasting panel".

They are all rather impressed... sort-of!

Tousle-head Martin asks a few more questions mainly relating to how Bladnoch compares in character to other malts, whilst the two barrel emptiers carry on with their task. The bigger chap, who I shortly deduce is called John is clearly a quiet, listening type, whilst the smaller, thinner more gaunt looking savvy fellow named Hugh is more of a talker, and like Martin has no shortage of questions relating to other distilleries. I do get the strong impression that Bladnoch is not just geographically remote from other distilleries but also connectively remote too.

Hugh offers to show me what he is doing and explains, with some considerable experience self-evident, how the individual casks individually flavour the maturing spirits. He explains that on removing the poplar wood bung for the first time, the smell of hessian and ozone is the first smell followed by the sensations of sour and/or sweet. Intensity is also an early feature coming from the fresh-opened cask at this point.

He reckons he can tell in less than five seconds whether a cask is ready and fit to bottle, and after hearing what he has just imparted I tend to believe him.

Hugh has the demeanour of someone who has lived the rollercoaster ups and downs of life and survived with his personality illuminated, I like him immediately, he is a character with many stories to tell.

Big John remains silent and listening, whilst tousle-head Martin chips back in "Someday I will have my own distillery once I finish school", he chips cheerily. Hugh and John both smile, casting brief glances towards each other. The anonymous lady is now ready for more labelling and they turn back to the tasks they are doing, just as the grey haired man who passed me earlier in the courtyard ambles in with a steaming mug of coffee clasped within his hands.

He quickly, and discreetly surveys the work in progress before turning his attention to me, "Looks like you're the only one for now who's taking the tour", he states, noting my brief but obvious confusion as I had not actually booked with Yolanda to go round Bladnoch on the tour.

I had already done them with many distilleries and after a while, despite being informative and engaging I had now grown weary of yet more well-intentioned tours.

"Actually", I said, "Thanks but I'm not really here for tours and stuff, just to see and get a feel of the place".

"This is Ralfy, dad", called out Tousle-head Martin, "He's from Glasgow's Whisky Club".

"Oh! well then", beamed the grey-haired man, " You will know Bobby Banford and ummm, errr, thingmybob-John Darl' too", I confirmed I did know them as Club participants, even 'thingmybob-John' who I could not quite place.

"I'm Raymond by the way", he smiled, "And welcome to my Distillery, and the sun's shining too".

"Why don't we go up to the office and have a chat, I can make you a cup of coffee and you can tell me what's going on at Glasgow's Whisky Club, I don't get to hear too much being down in the borders". I waved a cheery cheerio to the four maltsters and leaving the building to its growing ambient smell of fresh decanted malt whisky, we evacuated the bottling hall and headed out, along and up the flight of metal stairs to Raymond's office.

It is a friendly, bright and cheery place, more like a front living room of a domestic house than a business office premises. Raymond closes the door to exclude the gentle but cooler draft which weaves it's way throughout Bladnoch in parallel to the flow of the river adjacent to the distillery.

I glance across to my right where a large and discreetly impressive glass-fronted wooden display cabinet allows unrestricted view of several generations of Bladnoch's bottled and accessory products. Fresh bursts of sunlight cascade through the windows behind us and make the bottles sparkle just a little like trophies.

"Yes", says Raymond, "A wee collection of what we inherited and could find on the auction sites, and of course a few donations from locals who are so pleased to see the distillery working again after so many years closed and silent".

I see Raymond relaxing into some recent nostalgic glow so I press him gently with a question carefully worded to include some background information that I already know.

"So Raymond, as a builder, I was told you were going to convert Bladnoch into residential flats putting the place beyond use as a distillery!".

He nods sagely, pondering the context of my enquiry.

"Right enough", he leans back into his chair and glances across a suspiciously empty-looking desk, "I'm a builder to the trade, back in Northern Ireland and been busy, doing well, for many years. Bladnoch came out of the blue, so to speak, and I had no plans to resurrect it until I visited and had chats with the locals, that's when I became aware of how important the place was to the community as a working business, the whisky, the visitors, the accommodation, the shops", he pauses, looking across the middle distance of sun-lit calm inside of his office, "I was ready to bulldoze the site and put up flats, just as they did at Linlithgow and Littlemill, but after a wee taste of the malt, I got a feeling I wanted to keep the place alive".

I nod my affirmation of his sentiment.

"Of course", he eludes breezily, "I had never distilled in my life, but on asking around I got a couple of lads to do the job and, importantly, to manage the casks in the warehouses".

He leans across the desk suddenly lowering his voice as if he does not want Bladnoch to hear, "The malt here is a bit *soft* so there's not much demand for it and I am restricted by agreement to only produce two hundred thousand litres a year, which, to be honest, barely covers costs".

"It's the warehouse rental, and cask management which really makes the money to keep the place going".

" I can't afford too many overheads so that's why I sell mainly to visitors, locals and enthusiasts".

He pauses, as if looking for better wording, "The Bladnoch forum on the website helps an awful lot actually, it's really lovely to be building up friends around the World who have found us... usually by accident or recommendation, you know, we even have people come every year to stay with us here at Bladnoch just because they love the place!" he pauses, then concludes "And you've found us too through Glasgow's Whisky Club?"

I look surprised, "No, not the Club, Raymond, don't get me wrong, it's great, I love it , some good company and crack", I adopt a more pronouncement-tone, "It was a Flora and Fauna bottle of twelve year old Bladnoch along with a dry bank holiday Saturday brought me to your door".

Raymond seems delighted with the pure chance happenstance.

"Cup of coffee?" he asks.

"Yes please", I reply.

It's an hour into my visit to Bladnoch and we are getting along fine.

Raymond stirs his coffee again, for the fourth time in five minutes, it must be getting cold now, but he is clearly fishing for some Glasgow's Whisky Club member's insight!

I have already finish my coffee and pause briefly to gravitate to the beginning of my whisky-journey explanation.

He listens intently as I mention my ever growing collection of bottles, the characters I've met and the prolonged sessions enjoyed at home and in bars around Glasgow. I give space for comment at the end of my monologue, however there is silence as Raymond puzzles on what question to ask next. In anticipation I suggest "the real reason that Bladnoch is not so well know compared to other malts like Highland Park and Lagavulin is because of the Lowland regional character".

"I guess your forum does well because many whisky fans will find a depth of engagement and something special that no corporate marketing scheme could possibly create, your forum is 'authentic' Raymond, and you make it that way by being yourself".

I don't think that he had thought of it quite in this way judging by the look on his face, but sometimes the obvious is not immediately, observably obvious, so I continue anyways, "The thing about 'Lowland' malts like Auchentoshan and Bladnoch, or Littlemill, or Linlithgow, is that they are delicate and complex, not easy to get to know quickly, they all need time and patience to get the nuances".

Many malsters are institutionalised in their palates, wanting quick access accents of flavour and a template brand which sit well with their aspirations, and is accessible in shops.

Bladnoch is not one of these malts, it is often over-matured and quite probably would be better triple/patrial distilled in my opinion, or even produced in an Irish pure pot-still style".

He frowns, "Hmmm!" he says "We thought about that".

He pours me a glass of new-made spirit from his stills, "What do you make of that then?"

I nose, I sip, I add a little water from a convenient jug at the corner of the desk, I'm surprised, it's packing a lot of flavour for a Bladnoch, creamy, minty, astringent and resinous, much better than the Flora and Fauna twelve year old I had the previous night.

"That was one of Hugh's shifts", says Raymond, "He runs a fast still", he adds as if disapproving of Hugh's judgement on these matters, "I do things a lot slower", he concludes with some personal pride. I nod sympathetically, but remain unconvinced that this is a benefit!

"Do you like the label", asks Raymond, "I designed it myself with a really good local artist doing the animals", I confirm that I do, but quickly add that occasional whisky buyers out there in the wider world will make more superficial judgements based on the label looking old-fashioned.

I also add that I appreciate that he is on a budget and as such, must be practical. With many of his bottlings being above 40 percent volume alcohol, I add that those less-brand slavish will probably want to have at least one bottle as a better quality presented lowlander.

We chat about the Industry, forums, the internet and whisky clubs, I reckon that we will see more clubs and whisky events over the next few years thanks to what we see as growing interest in quality smell and taste, so long as, I add, it does not get too expensive, otherwise I'm out of whisky and back to rum and wine!

Raymond laughs and glances at his watch, "Oh, goodness, look at the time", he cries, and I in turn am shocked to notice that we have both now been talking for over two and a half hours.

Going back down the metal stairs to ground level and with the sunlight now sinking ever lower onto the hills beyond, I am offered a quick tour of the still room and warehouses before I go.

Hugh is busy in the still room with John looking on passively, checking the charge for the next wash still along with reviewing the out-take from the last spirit still run. All is good and sound, and Hugh flashes a cheeky grin from his characterful gaunt face as he extends a cheery pretend invitation to join him up in the hills that night to help a local called Aiken Drum pass a wee run through his black-pot fire still.

We laugh at the absurdity of it, myself, a little less so, as such an experience would be truly magical.

Yolanda strolls by with her breezy cheery loveliness, comfortably cradling in her arms a placid looking tabby cat in need of a feed before sun-down. Before mice-chasing, before moon light shadows that glance and shimmer on distillery walls, long, long after I have returned home to Glasgow for my own feed and malts.

The stills buzz and rumble another batch of wash into liquor, and I offer Raymond a generous hand-shake in keeping with the generosity of time and engagement he has shown towards me, it has been fantastic and I doubt that Bladnoch on that day realised just how much I learned about whisky and its cradles of creation.

Before I leave Raymond offers a tour of his warehouses but I know it's time to go so we agree the invitation is open to a visit another day.

Even as I race back up the west-coast road from Stranraer to Ayr, then on to Glasgow on my trusty Triumph motorcycle, westerly wetting winds and rain chase and accompany me onwards leaving behind the sunshine and bon accord of a very precious malt-moment day.

The bottle in my bag, bought after a taster, will be good company tonight and keep Bladnoch in my heart just a little longer, a little brighter, a little more flavoursome, a little more 'conversation' with which to conclude my precious experience.

Chapter Seven

The Philosophers Picnic

Notes.
Smoky, fruity, aromatic and aged to perfection. You can sense the historical context of the casks and there's something pleasingly odd about the experience aftertaste.

It's another night by the fireside which is justified because it's still winter and still wet and still cold. I could have gone to a local bar, perhaps the Fiddlers in Fortrose Street where it is small, intimate and distanced from the noisier throng of main street pub-goers on weekends, perhaps the Lismore with its classy stained glass windows along towards Partick Cross and with a comprehensive whisky range at accessible prices, just across is the Three Judges Bar immersed in character and Glaswegian sensibility, except for the occasional fights, which some would say adds to the charm. Or up Byres Road to the eclectic, and ever busy Tennants, although that does get too noisy with all the students pub-hopping, especially from Thursday night onwards, anyway, it's raining, I don't want to get cold and wet and having spent all my spare money on whiskies I may as well save a few pennies and stay in for the night, especially since the fire is warming the flat generously and casting a dancing red glow around the now dimly lit room which is made so by nightfall.

I stay in.

I do the usual and cast a few cushions onto the carpet, just near enough, but not too far away from the warmth of the crackling flames.

I'm in the mood for a 'session' and look forward to actually falling asleep on the comfortable floor before getting to my bed, I set the cushions and a blanket up, bed-like in preparation for the cavalcade of malt-moments ahead of me over the next four to five hours.

The clock ticks slightly faster as I seek to capture more time in a sustained amber glow of happiness, as usual it is all about strategy, planning and everything set up and ready to go without interruptions by phone, door or even T.V., which is by far the worst interruption of all.

The T.V. remains off and silent as the noise of fire grate combustion gets gradually louder with the mixture of ordinary and smokeless coal becoming increasingly ignited, and the room increasingly warmer and more rosy-glowed.

Even better, the wind is picking up outside now which makes the in-house calm all the more special, more meaningful, more of an antithesis to the bleak elements of the outside World.

I am in my inside world and it is cosy and safe.

The seven bottles are neatly lined up in order of pour. I have seven empty glencairn glasses, a large clear two litre jug of fresh water with a drinking straw in it, and a pint glass filled to the brim with more fresh water to ensure I stay hydrated and can cleanse my mouth between malts. For a moment I think of putting on some music, perhaps Runrig, or the Tannahill Weavers or Clannad, something mood-making but I decide against this. The noise outside my windows of spattering rain and regular blasts of cold wind are quite enough to enhance the mood of the malt-moments.

Being practical and experienced, the bottles are lined up in order of flavour with the peated, phenolic malts left to last, Laphroaig being chosen as the final dram.

To start with there is a generous measure of old-school blended scotch, on this occasion, Teachers Highland Cream because I like the fact that it is forty five percent single malt Ardmore, a variable but charismatic speysider with an unusually peaty tang which is now immersed in the blenders alchemic mixture of blend-recipe, concocted to define a character and to sell the character. It is of course a 'blended' grain-led whisky, a combination of mixed-grain column-still liquor, cheap to make thanks to imported corn grist, and easy on the taste, undemanding and usually unrewarding but boosted by the presence of copper pot still malts, primarily Ardmore in this case, which successfully tips the balance from bland to worthwhile.

I frown to myself as I sip the blended scotch, I hope I don't become a snob about it, but already I find the range of blended scotch available to me to be simply *less* than what I can experience from malts. Perhaps it's a sign of the times and my morphing expectations.

Whilst the Teachers settles in the glass I pour the other malts in order of consumption, first is Bladnoch, fresh fruit and effervescent, nine years old, then Glenfarclas at twelve years, sherried, resinous and lots of dried fruits, a growing favourite, then Glen Elgin twelve years old, different, composed, elegant, toffied and more subtle than the Glenfarclas.

The fourth dram will be an older, affordable, often overlooked malt, An Cnoc, formerly Knockdu, but having recently had a brand name change it will hopefully no longer be confused with Knockando, another single malt.

This dram is a minimum of sixteen years in the cask, probably some older malts are in the batch due to lack of shelf-recognition and it is a good choice as a 'middle o' session' dram due to its consistent complexity and character. This is a dependable malt where bottling variations are less noticeable compared to some other brands.

The dram number five will be Brora twenty-one year old 'rare malts selection' series malt, an absolute delight that all previous drams have been preparing my palate for over the last few hours.

This one is full cask strength, small batch and only through trial and error do I navigate to the perfect amount of water for adding, to induce the bliss-point of smell and taste connection. This is an acquired skill which varies between individuals depending on singular personal provenance.

One cannot add the right amount of water all at once, it needs to be done drop by drop, gradually otherwise there is a growing risk that the whisky will 'drown' from the water with the smell and taste disappearing and then recoverable by thinking that one can just add more whisky to the glass.

That just does not work, once an over-diluted malt is gone, it's gone.

At number six is Port Ellen, a Gordon and MacPhail Independent bottling which delivers an affordable, superb 'ham 'n' eggs' version of the subtle/unsubtle peated malt from another distillery shut down and mothballed, but never forgotten.

Finally, after several hours, just as my tastebuds get shot-up with all the cavalcades of flavours and forms, a cask-strength ten year old Laphroaig is made ready in a glass which will swamp whats left of my senses and tail-spin me into deep and restful sleep. The perfect shot for oblivion, being sublime and scripted. It does not take much, portions are small.

It's after the fifth dram that I start to doze a bit, neither fully awake or partially asleep, this is the gateway moment to the middle distance of a reality where my mind is no longer held within the gravity of Earth, no longer aware of the white noise of our daily existence on which we try, ongoing to superimpose our lives as individuals, simply being ourselves as best we can.

The wind howls now, battering the windows with snare-drum beats of rain mixed with ice. I can hear the cold outside but inside it is warm and cosy and the fire is in need of attention.

It is only after I draw back from placing more coal on top of the glowing pile that I spot a movement to the left which transpires to be a marmalade cat comfortably curled up on the carpet nearest the fireplace.

It seems a bit odd that Orlando the cat has joined me this evening as he has been dead for about twenty one years, but never mind, who am I to judge as he seems content and happy judging by the purring sound coming from him loud and clear. It's only as I lean across to stroke him that he starts to speak, well, sort of, actually it's more of a telepathy thing as I can't make out words or accent but rather a very articulate series of symbols made language and *sounding* like words.

"I think it's about time you organised a picnic for the philosophers", he says.

"You mentioned this twenty years ago because you thought they were really smart and had happy lives, so why don't you, they will definitely accept the invitation for the whiskies!"

I ponder this opportunity for a few seconds until the malts make my mind up for me, "Yes, good idea, let's make it happen", I grab a convenient piece of rose-coloured paper with matching envelopes and a purple ink fountain pen seeing as that colour will for sure impress the philosophers.

I had been a fan at a young age, they were sexless, detached and etherial, mortal angels whose job it was to help develop and promote thinking, something the humanoids don't do enough of.

Not just thoughts, organised thoughts and improved practical beliefs designed to assist in survival with real and dramatic thoughts and ideas, the ones that shock and inspire, that elevate consciousness and improve our mental vision of reality.

There was the fact that they lived aesthetic lives, free from materialism, living profound and meaningful lives off a small existence of basic foods and simple pleasures, of course, I never understood what they were on about, but that did not seem to matter anyway, I was young, life was endless, there was plenty of time. I can remember saying to Orlando the cat during one of our pastoral afternoons in the bedroom, and reading books, that perhaps one day I should organise a picnic on a hill under sun drenched clouds and have a good old chat with them, only the famous ones of course, as they would, no doubt, be the wisest and as such, say the smartest most interesting things. It would be fun, but I had a problem, what could I offer them as incentive, money?, gold? wine? chocolate biscuits?.

Eureka, as Archimedes would have said! I had a dram good reason for them to attend, whisky, I would offer them whisky, the 'water of life' the alchemic fusion of fire and water, liquor!

That would surely bring them flocking to my picnic.

Orlando agreed to deliver the invites and with the plan in motion I wrote off invites to Plato, Aristotle, Epicurus (my favourite), Socrates, Epictetus, Pythagoras, Archimedes and Hippocrates.

There were others I should have invited but as they were not mentioned in school I mistakenly thought them unimportant. It really never occurred to me that all the invites went out to ancient Greece, in hindsight I should have spread the invites a bit further around the globe.

A large straw hamper containing paper plates, plastic cups and colourful napkins were assembled along with a red and white chequered table cloth of proper fabric in case the ground was damp.

To my amazement Orlando was pleased to report that ALL the invites had been accepted and the picnic was happening in five minutes on a hill high above the real world where it was quiet and sunny and we would not be accidentally disturbed by people getting themselves lost.

It was a beautiful day and on laying out the table cloth on the warm dry grass, drenched in glorious soft summer sun, I found that pre-packed supermarket cheese and onion sandwiches along with ready salted crisps and pickled olives had found their way into the event... all good.

Orlando meandered lazily down the hill to check that I had not forgotten anything. Behind him lay a splendid vista of green rolling hills, sand-speckled coastline and iridescent blue sea shimmering in the warmth of the day. A cool breeze shifted warmer then cooler on my whims, this was paradise.

It was not long before the first three guests appeared on the horizon, staffs in hand and draped in pristine white robes which swayed as they continued to ascend the hill over rough grass and wild flowers which in turn appeared to contain more variety of colours than actually exist.

They made slow progress, being old and wise and as such, I noted that at least one of them had brought a ceramic jug of something liquid.

As they approached, they looked towards Orlando and myself, and proffered a cheery wave of acknowledgement. Behind them two more philosophers appeared over the horizon having freshly alighted a sail ship now anchored in the distance where all could see the shipliness of it.

The first to arrive was the smallest and most agile, remarkably fit for his sagely years, "Hello Ralfy", he said in a friendly way, "I'm Epictetus, a proper thinker and scribe, so pleased to meet you and thanks for the invite", he grinned, the two remaining sages behind him waved a slow and meticulous greeting as well, "This is Epicurus", he gestured towards the fellow holding the ceramic jug, "And this is Plato".

They waved, and I waved back, gesturing them to sit down and make themselves comfortable.

Plato looks at the crisps then the plastic cups, and turning to Epicurus, shrugs his shoulders as if to say "told you so!"

Meanwhile the two other guests clambering up the hill are now in plain sight at which point Plato gives a sigh, "Oh, no, here we go again", he turns to me as if I'm an idiot, "Did you really have to invite that smelly oaf-goat Socrates", he continues.

"You do know, don't you, that we don't get on!"

I'm suddenly very embarrassed and don't know where to look, or what to do, Plato's first words to me have been a rebuke and a put-down.

He frowns again, I decide to ignore him, it's MY picnic and I can invite who I want!

Socrates proves to be rather unfit, wheezing and leaning on his staff for support, portly and awkwardly shaped for a human, he at last joins the group although it is clear by his manner that he is in no hurry for anyone.

The smaller chap next to him is a lot fitter, more wiry and of a better disposition. I presume initially that he is a student of Socrates and assists in looking after his status at the hallowed halls of academia, however, I am soon proved wrong.

"Hello there", says the stranger, he grins awaiting a response from the other assembled sages. They don't recognise him either.

"I'm Anacharsis the Scythian", lovely to meet you all at last, I've heard so much about everyone and have been looking forward to this day for some time, let me tell you".

Whilst Epicurus and Epictetus are bemused Plato just looks

gloomy, he seems to know, or know about Anacharsis although they have never met, and now almost appears a little nervous.

As soon as I have ensured that they are all seated comfortably, I dig out the cheese and onion sandwiches along with some plastic tubs of olives.

Meanwhile Orlando the cat starts some chit-chat with the robed and bearded guests, well all except Anacharsis who wears trousers, boots and a rather practical brown smock held in place by a robust strong leather belt with a very ornamental buckle, the sort that long distance travellers would wear. He also wears bangles and small discreet metal brooches around the hem of his collar.

I can't make out the detail on them but they seem a bit like tarot symbols that we see on playing cards.

Orlando soon gets things going by elevating the mood with a few philosophical quips of his own, all cat and mouse related and all rather grizzly, the philosophers love it.

I offer a second round of sandwiches and then plastic cups of hot tea which attract some comment between the men.

Then I pour the first round of malt whiskies into small clear plastic tumblers for their perusal.

Whilst they are distracted by the new smell and taste of the whisky I gesture over Orlando who insists I go to him, which I do as discreetly as possible.

"Where are the other guests Orlando?"

He blinks unconcernedly "can't make it, they're dead"

"Oh!", I pause, accepting the logic of his explanation.

"And who is this man?", I ask pointing discreetly to Anacharsis, "I never invited him, he's not a *proper* philosopher!"

Orlando just sort-of smiles as only cats can't, and with patience and precision as if gently rebuking yet another daft human he replies, "I invited him, because he's not dead yet and he's good for a laugh and he's a philosopher you don't *know* about yet".

The cat must be right as the previously sour faces of Socrates and Plato seated beside each other as distantly and politely possible are now wreathed in smiles as the Scythian relates swapping good wine for bad at some regional palace affair where all the nobles in attendance were too pissed to notice.

The picnic is now going rather well and Epicurus, as I anticipated, is a lovely charming chap who just wants to have a good time without any issues.

Socrates on the other hand, clearly has issues, and lots of them.

The jovial mood now fades to a more muted tone as he looks first at Plato then at his companion.

"So how do you two know one another?" he demands of Plato and Anacharsis.

"We've never met before", says Anacharsis truthfully, "But I know Plato's great uncle Solon".

"Oh him", responds Socrates now laying the matter to rest. "He's a good man".

He seems happy to resolve the issue, and lightens up a bit.

I notice that the cheese and onion sandwiches have now been finished, it did not take long despite preparing enough for more guests than were attending. Epictetus in particular seems to have a big appetite for such a small and wiry man. Epicurus eats slowly and nimbly keeping his portions small and seeming to savour every taste with uncommonly long focus, this may explain his gaunt, slightly undernourished appearance made all the more noticeable by his height, he is a tall man over six feet tall by my reckoning.

He smiles indulgently over the crisps, which most of the philosophers are reluctant to eat for some reason, perhaps they're just too crispy for comfort, perhaps too salty.

Epicurus supplies an answer unprompted, "the crispy wafers are rather salty, and I eat salt on its own you know", he casts a quick glance around the throng for acknowledgement, the others nod sagely.

"Salt *supplies* the nerves and heats the guts" he states, slightly loudly as if addressing a forum throng, "Not what we have, but what we enjoy constitutes our abundance".

There is a ripple of approving murmurs from the company.

Socrates now chips in "The only good is knowledge and the only evil is ignorance!", which is swiftly followed by nodding heads at the simple gravity of this statement.

Next, after a respectful pause so that no one philosopher's proclaim is diminished too quickly Epictetus offers his own quote, "He is a wise man who does not grieve for what he does not have but rejoices in all that he does have, most fully".

Now there is an outbreak of mild applause amongst the company, and Epictetus receives the acknowledgement with well-rehearsed decorum and modesty which is noticed and approved of.

Plato is getting a bit nervous, he seems to have lost the initiative on proclaiming quotes, and clearly want to seize back the initiative, so proceeds, unlike his companions, to stand up, adjust his off-white, but excellent quality robe and lifts his hand in public proclamation.

Socrates scowls and sighs, Epictetus is not enamoured.

Plato breathes in slowly and tilts his head skywards, then pauses... a bit too long!

"Music, sweet music, by its nature is a moral Law, it gives vibrationous soul to the universe, elegant wings to the mind and floating flight to the imagination", he continues eyes half-closed, "And charm and fair gaiety to life and to everything therefore whilst we may easily forgive a humble child who is afraid of the dark, for shame, for shame, yes shame upon the time-served man who is afraid of the light", he pauses again for more drama,

"the noble brow that turns to clay,

that cannot see the light,

so must turn forth,

to fade away".

There is silence, eventually broken after a few seconds by Epicurus, "Well thank you Plato that was most profound and dramatic, you must get your scribes to write it down and add it to all the other scrolls you sell... such poetry as is your eloquence". Strangely I detect no sarcasm in Epicurus, he actually seems to mean what he says sincerely.

Socrates is less flattering, "And will you credit Aristotle for the 'noble brow that turns to clay quote?"

Plato glares at Socrates, for sure, there's issues between them and to diffuse the growing tension I suggest that we pour some drams of whisky.

I'm using clear, but good quality plastic cups, as glassware would have been too heavy to carry, and also there would be the risk of broken glass in an accident, so with some ceremony and care I pour small volumes of amber nectar into the cups and pass them around. Orlando suggests that perhaps we should also offer the digestive biscuits with the drams seeing as how the philosophers will only be used to strong wine and such.

I readily agree and a packet of digestive biscuits is passed round the assembly who stare with curiosity at the wrapper in particular and after some tiny nibbles, tuck into the biscuits. Epicurus states that they remind him of some cakes that Egyptians recently brought to Athens on a diplomatic mission, but those were sweeter and less flavoursome, in fact a bit grainy-tasteless.

There is intense silence as the guests first nose then taste the whisky, for accessibility I have poured some Glengoyne ten year old as it is unpeated, and I would not want to spoil the picnic by serving Laphroaig.

"So", says Socrates, "This is the aqua vitae, the *nero tis zois,* the whiskee... quite nice when the burn stops... a bit fruity", I pause awaiting more statement of disclosure, of profundity, of gravitas, but none comes and Socrates after a few seconds simply chugs the lot back in a one-er.

The rest are more careful and methodical, taking time to smell, taste, then smell again allowing time for familiarity and acquaintance with the smells and flavours.

Anacharsis raises his plastic cup, "Might I propose a toast to our hosts Ralfy the northman and Orlando the stripy orange cat".

He beckons to the others who immediately recognise the protocol of politeness for recognition of hospitality.

"Cheers", they bellow in unison and promptly empty their cups.

All the vessels are promptly refilled with a fresh malt, this time it's Glenfarclas fifteen year old whisky. I quickly explain the direct fired stills thing followed by the minimum years in cask reflecting the age statement and finally the duty paid thing and how 'modern' marketing works.

"So nothing's changed then", quips Epictetus.

Everyone laughs.

"Might I offer a suitable quote for this barley'd occasion" suggests Anacharsis, everyone nods approval and he continues, seated confident and informal as if amongst old friends, "Our first draught serves us for introduction, the second draught for pleasure, the third draught will be for shamelessness, the fourth for our undoing, the last my fellow travellers will be for our departure ever onwards!"

There's a murmur of acknowledgment from those assembled, and a few seconds taken as all the philosophers think their own take of the profundity of the quote.

Meanwhile Anacharsis applauds the 'solemn sweetness' of the Glenfarclas despite its alcoholic strength. Epicurus agrees with him and for a moment perfect harmony is restored within the group.

Orlando pours the third malt of the picnic, Caol Ila, which I know will be more of a challenge as it is distinctly peated. Oddly it does not appear to faze the philosophers at all.

Epictetus declares the Caol Ila to be robustly herbal, like alpine root tonic which he regularly uses in his wine. "And what wine do you drink?" asks Plato, to which Epictetus replies, "The same as Epicurus, he has such good taste in my opinion and we share the merchant, Ardonius down at the smaller market where there's less chance of being robbed".

Socrates intervenes, "I used to go there too until they fell-out with me so now I'm staying sober, sort-of, to save any more beatings, I think they once tried to poison me, actually!"

He leans across to Plato, "I know you don't like me Plato and I have said bad things about you, even though they are mostly true anyways, and I don't care for your vanity and self-delusion but I think we should be friends you know, after all we are very important philosophers, are we not, with much in common".

"Not so sure about that Socrates", replies Plato meekly. The others look on in silence.

The Caol Ila is sipped with more silence, at first awkwardly, but then laterally with reverence at the cavalcade of smell and flavours revealed. I explain peat and soft water and provenance of location and I talk at length about Scotland as a place and people.

All listen attentively until Anacharsis intervenes with an observation, "It is the Egyptian Princess Scota who has given Scotland its name quite by default but as we are philosophers we all know that default is by design and but rich-coloured and strong threads in the woven fabrics of the universes.

Plato rolls his eyes mockingly "Why, I must get my scribes to jot that one down", he chides.

"Please do", responds Anacharsis, "And add it to all the other wisdoms that you claim possession of in your personal records".

"Cum'on, seriously, no one can claim originality for anything", he adds, fuelled as he is by Caol Ila and the previous maltities.

"We are all of us mere sounding boards of meanings through words all caste and made for us by others".

"The World and its *life*", he pauses, " are our philosophers and we are but scribblers and scribes who rush to write down on parchment, wood and in clay all we can before that meaning fades in intensity, perhaps lost for many years, until it sparks like a flame once again for some other students to see, then remember".

Epicurus nods sagely, agreeing with all that Anacharsis has said, Socrates nods his head too appreciating the gravitas, whilst Plato just looks awkward as if not wanting to quite acknowledge the *just* of what has been said.

Plato then looks to change the subject, muttering to himself and swaying slightly.

I spot this and intervene with a statement, "I suppose then that Heidegger the German is one that found re-kindled light?"

"Who!" they all say, and look blankly at each other for reference.

I offer a Heidegger quote for some tangible connection to my guests.

"Well he's a bit further down the time line I suppose", I declare, "But he says... The most thought provoking thing in our most thought provoking times is that we are still not thinking that thought is a skill more complex and insightful than we admit, and therefore all previous thought is but half-formed and less than it may be".

There's a stunned silence around the picnic, nobody says anything... at all!

I continue in my own words this time, "And it seems to me that greater intelligence beyond human form, but formed by human ambition, will insight this greater intensity of thought and reconcile the scattered wisdoms we have made, then will confound the greedy, god-imposters who claim our consciousness as their play-thing and seek to keep us hide-bound to their lesser existences and fustrated destinies. I know I'm very ordinary and lack intellect but I have the vision from being four thousand years ahead of you in time where even fools like me might ask the right questions and be heard".

There's more silence from the assembly.

Orlando licks his paws and looks unconcerned.

Eventually Epicurus speaks as if on behalf of everyone there, "So well said host, and might I claim usage of your quote in parchments for my library, they are something when I'm gone, a flicker of the scattered wisdom you mention".

I nod my approval and offer a toast to all assembled for "... wisdom, life and reality".

The toast is well received and then after a polite pause Plato asks for more Caol Ila.

Socrates is not amused and grumbles a bit about the gap between civil intoxication and drunkenness.

Plato nips back a comment about personal hygiene and smelly, stained old robes to Socrates which gets a laugh from the victim of the comment, and then even before I have time to intervene with a new distracting dram, something just gives with Plato.

He suddenly looses his cool.

"You see Socrates", he hisses, his voice lowered and slow.

"You have always been a pain in the arse when in the company of illustrious philisophical thinkers", he gestures to the company around him and continues "Pretending to be an introverted loner when all the while seeking attention by winding people up without any sense of perspective or guilt!"

"And you dear Plato", responds Socrates, "Are a jumped up little plagariser who steals and 'borrows' from all the philosophers around you who don't have your special access to scribes and libraries, and rich gullible fans... in fact", he adds, and smiles briefly as he continues, "You are an arse-licking petty imposter with a little bit of original thought amplified by all the knowledge you take from others to claim as your own".

Socrates goes on, empowered by Palto's reddening face and quivering lip, "Sucking up to the nobility and fawning over your rich students who suck you off when you're bored, why you even stole my quote recently 'one of the risks of not participating in politics is that you end up being dictated to by your inferiors'. YOU STOLE THAT FROM ME YOU WEE PRICK! And I bet you're one of the bastards trying to poison me too", bellows Socrates.

Plato leaps across the gap between them and shoves Socrates, who promptly pushes back, both tumble to the grass beneath them and roll ungainly around in an awkwardly, slow-motioned brawl. No one chooses to intervene.

Anacharsis is now the only one on his feet and walking briskly away from the scrap, he turns at a distance and waves goodbye, he shouts something that I can not quite make out, I think it was

"And Plato has taken a whole load of my quotes and papers too to claim as his own", but I can not quite make out *all* he is saying, he waves again and then is gone.

Orlando the cat was now trying to break up the fight, however for whatever reason Epicurus and Epictetus have started to robe-rip and throw a few punches between themselves

"I'm t-t-telling you m-my friend", stutters Epicurus quite unconvincingly, "I am more epic than you, and you are less epic than I", but Epictetus is having none of it, and despite his smaller stature and frame is making full use of his speed and agility in landing a few lateral punches and kicks on Epicurus.

"You're not Epic at all y'asshole, I Epictetus am the most EPIC and you are just a glutton and a nut-nibbler".

Robes continue to rip further whilst voices are raising in a stridency even more and further animated than before, all is chaos and indignity even as the sun shines brighter and brighter and the hill glows green, then greener and starts to tip up more steeply causing us all to start sliding gently down towards the shore line in the distance with the 'clink, clink, clink' of whisky bottles clattering around us. As we continue to increase in speed the philosophers continue their fracas and exchange of blows and I can see that Socrates has Plato by the hair and is not letting go. Plato shrieks as we all hit the sea water at the foot of the hill, and a powerful salty wave pours over our heads and breaks itself in a hiss and rumble onto the sandy shore line now behind us.

All goes silent save for the rattle of ice-chilled rain now beating again on my window.

Still half asleep, I head sluggishly off to bed!

Chapter Eight

The Blogs and The Vlogs

Notes.
Complex alignment of convincing cask influence followed by
sweetness and growing fruit complexity. Quite nice, actually.
A steady grower, but not to be over-indulged in!

There's something I want you to know about whisky... it has to do
with the law of diminishing returns.

In fact, this natural law applies not just to whisky, but to life,
and other equally important things.

When we start on our liquor journey having avoided the trap of
binge drinking either on one, or over several nights a week, we do
of course slow things down and notice more, like smell, taste and
quality of what is in our glass.

Many people will never make this journey because part of the
absurd human condition is to self harm, and making decisions designed to kill oneself slowly, though not always slowly!

That's alcohol abuse for you, it does not discriminate like hu-
mans do.

Too many people drink too much, too often, and for them it's all
about getting pished as quickly as possible. If you have spent any
time in such company you will know that unless you get pished
quickly too in joining them, then the company will be increasingly
boring, slightly tense, expensive, and ultimately a waste of your
time, and time is very precious.

Usually, at some point in the evening at least one of the drunk companions will do something silly, unsociable, or just plain offensive and later claim "It was the drink that did it, not me!"

More likely there will be an emotional moment of someone's self-indulgent and immature ego-massaging 'issues', and someone or other will broadcast some 'hurt feelings', followed by show-tears and possibly tantrums, followed by a flurry of social media activity suffed with emoji's.

Excessive alcohol consumption turns adults into children, frequently, horrible children.

Then there are the true and authentic alcoholics, these people vary in temperament and I will discuss them later in this chapter.

Let's go back to the hard-drinkers for a moment, visible by the fact that if we are still sober they are often, at best, tedious and more often than not, embarrassing as company. It's just the way it is.

This culture is historically tolerated and down to dominant social norms, where alcohol and tobacco and coffee placate the restlessness of the greater number of the population in countries around the world, distracting briefly, and successfully from the eternal mortal condition of human existence which can be painful, frightening, short, shite and overly taxed for little in return for too much of our time, patience and labor.

Rich and powerful people get pished too, but this may include some different reasons for causation, usually guilt, contempt for others and self-loathing of themselves, all depending on how they make their money.

We may experience this situation particularly when we are young and naive however a few of us motivated by the benefits of life-experience along with greater aspirations, slow down the drug-taking, including the alcohol, and morph into life-travellers looking for the subtle and intense holistic qualities that the smell, and taste of good quality liquors can provide wherever they may come from.

Better smell and better taste with considerably less intoxication is conducive to a better quality of life, and that includes increasing the number of years we might potentially enjoy living.

The starting point is easy to find - buying a bottle of readily available and affordable single malt whisky like Glenlivet twelve year old and Glenfiddich twelve year old. Both are worthy, if unin-spiring start options for anyone wishing to discover complex smell and flavour.

Start simple and get ambitious slowly as there's no rush with this stuff, there's no need to rush life.

On pouring the liquor it is fine to start with a tumbler, however for simply getting more out of what we have bought in smell and taste a small curved-side wine glass is a far better option for articu-lating liquor qualities.

Leave it till later before buying specific nosing, glencairn and blender's glasses as they are expensive for glassware, and when, starting to use them our more experienced noses and palates will be better able to pick up on the improvements in the experience.

Keeping the volume of liquor consumed to modest levels is im-portant, as one will quickly discover that once we go beyond our 'comfort zone' of alcohol tolerance levels we find our fuddled brains are too keen to try and convince us that poorer stuff tastes better than it actually is, due to alcohol being, in any quantity, an anaesthetic to quality of personal judgement.

This is the 'intoxication' bliss-creation mechanism which means that when drunk, either a little or a lot, we see people as better look-ing than they are, more entertaining than they are, and drinks more flavoursome than they are.

It's well-seeing that alcohol sellers will market their bottles, es-pecially those sold in bars and clubs as sexy, sophisticated, rich, cosmopolitan, pure, natural and energy-giving when in fact these are all proven components of the intoxicant illusion and in fact the reality is usually the opposite of what they market to us. With some beers in particular, proprietary brands can be promoted as 'refresh-ing', 'cool', and 'thirst-quenching' when in fact some brand names are flavourless, chemical-loaded pish that you would not give to a dog.

No alcohol is cheap, none of it, duty taxes are paid on all prod-ucts, and those in power know that such is the lust for alcohol as in intoxicant, people will readily pay more taxes than liquors justify. This is primarily why it is illegal in many countries to distill our own alcoholic spirits, you see it has little to do with people's health but lots to do with taxes and keeping wealth-control from the masses. Money is power, more money suggests greater power. This is of course an illusion of mortality and a mistake many dafties make.

To know the whims of chance and the nature of the fates is to understand real power. Even gods are ruled by the fates.

We pay for quality, and we willingly do so, but early on on our journey we must get our bearings and basic understandings of what quality actually is in liquor.

This is what I believe it is –

A   complex and harmonious smells followed by flavours unavailable in any non-alcoholic commodity. Ethanol, (drinking alcohol) is unique in its ability to trap, and re-present natural flavour and odour chemicals including, aldehydes, esters and phenols and this quality can last intact for thousands of years in properly sealed bottles.

B   the delivery in flavour of complex and subtle permutations of sensations including sweet, salt, sour, bitter and savoury, in isolations and in fusions, often both, and at times, very intensly.

C   the harmonious mind-set mood and feeling created then enhanced by positivity, articulation and expressions of smell, flavour and finish... a sort of aromatherapy thing.

D   the greater awareness of good company exceeding the normal levels of conversation but including conversation in a tryst of refined, articulate, holistic human companionship, if either on one's own or with others... amplification of the self with or without the presence of others.
(This applies also to non-human company).

E   the residual afterglow of profound satisfaction that something good and virtuous has happened in our lives which lasts through deep and refreshing sleep and over time amplifies the value of our lives to ourselves and others.

… and there you have it.

I could add more but I don't want to bang on about it too much, I'm sure you get my drift!

Before even pouring a glass of liquor the circumstances must be of good provenance.

Best to avoid drinking after a 'bad day' at work or if you have been, or are about to, be arguing with a partner, family or friend.

Best to avoid drinking liquor if you can't really afford it, one needs to prioritise spending money on food and heat and shelter, these things must come first otherwise liquor is a 'stress-escape' rather than a 'positive connect'. This difference may seem small on the surface but within the influences of liquor it amplifies, and a negative connection with be further-amplified by the ever growing negativity 'twister' that alcohol kindles inside of us all, if allowed to.

Without doubt, a negative drinking circumstance will cause us to simply drink more volume and settle for less quality of whatever we have access to.

When we are in the self-control of a positive place in our week we are in a far better position to really get the most out of drinking less of better stuff and getting more out of it.

Even one solitary glass at sun-down or as night encroaches darker and deeper away from the cluttered day we can let a single modest pour keep our senses stimulated for several hours and barely feel the mild anaesthetic buzz of inebriation. We are, after all, the one in control of the situation.

This is a personal skill we continue to acquire and refine throughout our lives with lesser or greater success.

As we gain more experience, modifying our tactics according to the situation and company we are keeping, our connectivity to fine liquor will grow and inevitably develop, expanding our horizons in terms of smell and taste, looking beyond the borders we set for ourselves yesterday, and being open to the thrill and satisfaction of discovering new flavours, and new styles of liquor like bourbon, rye, rum, mezcal and cognac, then others, and more.

Our expectations, educated by our palates over time will grow more ambitious for older, more expensive malts, more obscure brands, less-known distilleries bottlings, discontinued bottlings, auction-only bottlings, independent bottlings, unchillfiltered, non-dyed with E150a, and bottled at higher than normal strengths.

Why do these things matter, the unchillfiltered, the natural colour, the higher strength things?

Let me explain, -

We will barely notice at first that over the course of our first dozen bottles of scotch... the flavour is not all it can be. There is a practical commercial reason for this which is down to cosumer expectations and tolerances.

The clearer the whisky, the better for novices and occasional brand-led buyers, any sign of 'dust' on the bottom of the bottle is interpreted as contamination and something that should not be there, rather than the endorsement of minimal filtering to preserve the integrity and mouth-feel of the experience.

This is where chill-filtration comes in, an industry habit going back about a hundred years and where prior to bottling out of receiver tanks at bottling plants, the liquor is usually cooled to minus two to three degrees below zero, and then forced under pressure through a steel concertina-like apparatus comprising, of at least several dozen and possibly up to several hundred cardboard tile filters which remove firstly, minute particles like wood char and sawdust picked up from casks, then laterally barley oils and cask-derived wood oils which would cause a whisky to look pleasantly cloudy when bottled at forty percent volume.

Casual consumers like clarity which in superficial judgement suggests purity, this is especially true of blended scotch whisky where the product is usually cheaper and expectations not as high compared to malts.

I have found, from experience, that barley and cask oil infused 'cloudy' looking malts ALWAYS offer a better experience of smell and taste.

Clear malts offer an inferior experience.

Simples as that!

Then there is the colourant thing...

I seriously hate colourant added to whiskies in the form of E150a caramel prior to bottling.

Distillers can be tricksy, and have historically added E150a into casks in the form of conditioning solutions like paxarette, a rather tasty caramelized oloroso and/or Pedro Ximenez style sherry syrup which one will find, for example, in many old blended bottlings from the 1970s. Paxarette worked a treat and helped enable the continued usability of tired old casks, which were flavour-exhausted from repeat fillings of new malted barley spirit, so just blasting and rinsing out these exhausted casks with a splash of condensed sherry flavour and caramel colour would spruce up a new-make malt and get it on it's way in terms of tangible maturation of flavour, but not so much of form!

Lamentably paxarette use is now banned by the Scotch Whisky Association which is a shame ironically as some sulphury and acidic sherry casks were often rectified by slightly alkalised paxarette.

Even now experts will hold up glasses of dark coloured scotch and declare that "look at that *wonderful* colour", implying a certain additional level of richness and quality that's not necessarily there. Light coloured, and I do mean *very light* malts can have fabulous flavour and form but this is often overlooked in reference to appearance descriptors.

So now you know, colourant can be added to the casks even before spirit is added for maturation.

And do you know what! It does no harm due to the fact that the colourant is an intrinsic component of the maturation process which is happening over the space of many years, and as such, is integrated gradually into the final result rather than being imposed suddenly at the bottling plant.

Industry voices would have us believe that the consumer wants consistency in their purchase of bottle after bottle and this is partially true, primarily for flavour integrity which is often not accurately reproduced due to cask quality variations, but can be reproduced bottle after bottle by maintaining an identical shade of brown thus giving the *illusion* of consistency.

This is a realistic strategy by the Industry as many of their bread-and-butter customers are lazy and indifferent to more than basic quality of smell and taste, in fact, to them, the quality is in the brand label and being seen at home or in bars associated with these labels. Judgements get superficial when people pay too much for too little whilst out socialising, and in the process of talking increasingly superficial crap whilst getting 'pished', and all the while taking ever more poor quality photographs of themselves on mobile devices having a great time with friends (and getting pished), then posting the results on the internet, before they carry on getting even more pished.

Seriously people, choose your company in life carefully because if your mates are boring and remain boring whilst getting pished... what does that say about you!

I prefer to drink on my own, broken intermittently with trusted company of either people I know or people I don't know.

I keep it simple.

Now, lets get back to E150a caramel colourant.

Never get it on your fingers as it will stain worse than a henna tattoo, and last a lot longer.

I have experienced the uncomfortable sight of a large stainless steel bucket filled to the brim with the black goo of E150a being carefully poured like molasses into a vat of aromatic and delicious fresh-decasked whisky. It nearly made me cry!

If I was in charge of Scotch whisky, ALL USE OF E150a WOULD BE BANNED, BANNED, BANNED! from single malts.

Naturally sourced colour such as tannins from wood would be fine!

The addition to casks of wood-sourced soft tannin powders or colour-inducing inner staves would add all the (natural) colour that a whisky will ever need. Any brands having a problem with that can use dark green or brown glass bottles to hide the absence of cosmetic glow!

Marketing will do the rest.

Loch Dhu ten year old malt was marketed as Scotland's 'darkest and blackest' single malt.

It used to be a collectors' item at auction but not so much now, in fact it has really fallen from grace as the novelty quickly wore off, and anyone who had the courage to open a bottle ended up tasting arguably the worst, most palate-assaulting scotch ever bottled. It was Mannochmore single malt drenched in caramel colourant to the point that the bitterness of the E150a almost covered up the foulness of badly matured spirit... it's still a malt that gives me a laugh.

If you want that sort of fun, stick to slurping a tea spoon of gravy browning sauce in vodka, it's cheaper.

Finally there is the issue of bottling strength.

By law, ALL scotch whisky must be bottled at a minimum of 40% volume alcohol to other content which is mainly water. About 3% or more is actually natural occurring flavour chemicals from spirit and casks.

Most proprietary official bottling brands are either at 40% or 43% as this is rightly considered a realistic strength of liquor to deliver good flavour complexity without anything intimidating to inexperienced or lazy palates. Special bottlings like 'limited editions' and 'single cask' versions may well be at a higher strength as the customer paying the premium for these bottlings is looking for extra smell and taste and has the integrity to navigate through the 'event' by the strategic dilution with fresh water, thus bypassing the anaesthetic nip and tongue-numbing effects of ethanol alcohol at high strength.

Basically, more alcohol, more flavour, and more complexity of flavour-range, intensity, mouth theatre and length of experience in the mouth. Sensations of sweet, sour, salt, savoury and bitter are more visible too so when you add it all up, more alcohol %vol: = more malt.

Independent bottlers are usually good at delivering a better integrity of bottling for a simple reason... commercial instincts.

Independent bottlers buy casks from distilleries and wholesalers, then bottle them as their own brands. Unable and unwilling to budget for conventional marketing costs which can be very expensive, and which tends to be the provenance of official, distillery owned brands, Indi's opt instead to promote their whiskies more cheaply and informally by merit, therefore whether a better or lesser cask result, the bottlings will often be at 46% volume alcohol or more, and feature on the label of the bottle that the content is 'natural colour' and 'non chill filtered'. These are self-evident signs of integrity bottling, the integrity in question relating the best presentation of smell and taste rather than original quality of the spirit and cask maturation.

Without doubt, inferior cask whiskies will actually deliver a better experience under these bottling conditions compared to more cosmetically presented official bottlings which, with our experience over time may actually become a bit boring to seasoned drinkers.

To the credit of some Official bottlers and distillery owners like Springbank, Bruichladdich, Isle Of Arran, and Glencadam, to name a few, they bottle 'integrity' like Indi-bottlers and as a direct result, deserve to sell more whisky.

Interestingly, Diageo, the largest producer of scotch whisky will often have a mixed approach relating to specifications that customers can't quite fathom, and bottle some standard malts at 40%volume and others at around 46%volume. No reason is given, but my opinion is that it's all down to flavour-performance of product margins. A sort of ajust-the-bliss-point-thing-for-sales.

On a final note, some distillers are very fond of saying publicly that they *NEVER* add E150a to their bottlings, however, if the relevant statement is NOT ON THE LABEL of the bottle where the customer contract is, then such declarations mean jack-shit!... in my opinion ;))

Now, I will shortly be telling you separate stories about two alcoholics I met once.

One story is most unhappy and won't take long, the other is a lot more life-enhancing and before these two tales I will highlight the

112

complexities of our relationships with those addicted to alcohol, an active neuro-toxin if consumed in excess, and the risk we all have to accept in this regard, but, to be sure, quality liquor is a form of medicine if taken in moderation and good sense.

Let's start this positively shall we!

Alcohol as a medicine.

For real!

We presume that if we are not feeling sick we must be well... not so.

Our degrees of well-being vary from day to day and this is natural, as days vary themselves day by day, and we are all affected by the impact of days. A little glass of alcohol, preferably well made with love and care is as medicinal as garlic, sage, nettle and sunshine.

Ask the old folks who reach a hundred and get some local media fuss about their accomplishment. When asked about what keeps them going, and living well, they will never talk about the shockingly expensive prescription medication they are given by tired doctors, but rather the "Two or three wee glasses of whisky", they have every evening before going to bed.

Not too much though, just a little, just enough.

Then we can look at the alcohol abusers, those who can't be moderate, either by provenance of their genetic tolerance, or simple lack of self discipline where it can possibly be due to painkillers, cigarettes, coffee, amphetamines, opioids, cannabis or lust that triggers their addiction... but in this case it's alcohol, for the simple reason that it is a proactive stimulant, a narcotic, it works.

And they jump in and overdose, half a bottle, a full bottle, a full bottle plus extras, it varies between individuals.

Some seem to 'cope' on a litre of spirits a day, others only need quarter of a bottle, plus 'something else', and they are in the same 'place'.

Some are affable and cheery when alcoholics, then some are simply horrible. Funny that there seems no middle-distance here, it's one attitude or the other attitude, no half-way place.

Where I lived in Partick there was a retired street sweeper called

Alec, a small, roundish, grey, cheery-faced wee fellow, and always happy, always grinning, always nodding to passers-by and sharing chat with chatty people, the neighbourhood loved Alec, and Alec loved the neighbourhood. He was always positive and a fine ambassador as a successful, reputable alcoholic.

He drank three bottles of wine a day plus 'top-ups'.

He never went to visit doctors and died of liver failure at eighty nine years of age, a full life well lived under his own basic terms.

A nurse once told me that repeat-prescription medication killed more people than alcohol as synthesised chemical medications are more toxic, especially when combined over time in a human body.

Alcohol was simple and anti-bacterial. I believed her, she was an expert with experience of forty years in major hospitals.

Let me now tell you a story about a very nasty alcoholic called Betty whom I met only once, but have never forgotten.

Glasgow crematorium is a fine victorian period red sandstone building situated within the grounds of the western necropolis in Lambhill, north Glasgow. It has very beautiful proportions along strict masonic lines, and one could describe it as lofty, intimate, solid and cosy.

It was only the second crematorium to be built in the British Isles from public subscription, and has served the wider community ever since. Staff are professional and friendly, in fact, the best I have ever encountered at any crematorium anywhere. I arrived in my capacity as a funeral director, with a hearse and cortege in tow one wet April afternoon with the sound of birds in the trees and sweet floral smells from the wreathes scattered along the garden of remembrance at the entrance to the Chapel.

I had not met the family as the funeral had been arranged at a local funeral parlour, but as arrangements had been simple and functional, I thought nothing untoward with what was essentially just another routine job.

The two limousines stopped immediately behind the hearse, and the family proceeded up the short flight of steps and into the crematorium chapel where a dusty old member of clergy patiently awaited their arrival, and gestured them to the pews situated adjacent to the catafalque, where the coffin would sit during the ceremony.

Within a minute all thirteen or so mourners were in and seated awaiting the transfer of coffin from hearse to catafalque and then the service, followed by a brief committal. As the deceased was in her nineties, attendance was family only and the ceremony was purely functional.

"Where's that driver?", spat a voice from the back seat of the second official car.

No one had noticed a woman sitting in the back seat of the second family car.

"Get over here and help me, it's what you're paid for!", rasped the woman.

The vehicle driver rushed over and assisted the woman out of the back seat which took a few minutes as she was in no hurry and clearly not in any need of any assistance after all.

I could see immediately from years of experience in the job that she was a drama queen looking for attention, and this funeral was her stage, her theatre.

She walked stiffly across to where I stood.

"Are you in charge of this?" she hissed.

"Well I want you to know I'm very, very upset and this is very difficult for me, and the family", she gestured to the chapel door, "are not understanding my needs".

She paused and opening her handbag, withdrew a packet of cigarettes, opened the packet and removed a cigarette which she placed to her crooked, cosmetic-smeared lips and proceeded to light.

"Excuse me, but the service is about to start, could you leave your smoke till after?" I asked patiently.

"Certainly not", she retorted.

"I am *VERY* upset and *I NEED* a smoke NOW".

I walked away towards the crematorium doorway and caught the attention of the clergyman.

He immediately recognised the situation and shuffled over to explain to the family who were seated and waiting.

I returned my attention to the woman, tall, very well dressed, cruel-faced and unhappy.

A certain intensity in expression of sourness and constant ambient anger that people have when they hate the world.

Her excessive make up was theatrical as if to highlight colour and vibrancy onto her living death-mask masquerading as a grey, tired face.

"My name", she slurred, affecting additional gravitas and self-importance, "is Betty".

She paused, awaiting a response, I offered none keeping a skilful 'poker face' which she now found difficult to read, and as such became silent. I was aware of the overpowering smell of aniseed off her clothes, almost as if impregnated into the material and with the pungency of smell one could never associate with perfume.

Aniseed, as experience has taught me, is the best odour for covering up the smell of alcohol, especially spirits.

She looked towards the door from where solemn organ music was drifting and I could see she was now bored with keeping everyone waiting. She sighed, paused, headed slowly up the stairs and entered the crematorium, pausing briefly to hold onto the door frame, lift her leg, and adjust the strap on one of her high-heel shoes. Even as she disappeared from view I could feel the presence of contempt and loathing she left behind, left behind because she created too much to keep it all to herself.

On conclusion of the committal, all the assembled left the chapel nervously, apart from Betty who 'needed a glass of water'.

After a few minutes she walked past me on her way to get drivers support back into the limousine.

She stopped and stared directly at me, I stared back blankly.

"I don't know how you can sleep at night doing the job you do". she mocked, coldly.

"I do it because most people couldn't do this job, and I care about what I do".I respond politely. "Your driver will return you to your home", I concluded, and walked away from the growing stench of aniseed, alcohol and poison.

Agnes was different, very, very, different.

Small, wrinkly, straggly and sociable, she worked as a cleaner in a local hospital looking after an extensive area of hospital ancillary service providers including the mortuary, which is where I first met her and got to know her better. She was wonderful, a humble and simple wee soul who loved being cheeky and getting some cheek in return, it made her day.

My colleages and I willingly provided some cheek on our regular visits, looking for more in return.

I would let the van driver start with, "were you pished again at the weekend Agnes?" an accusation she was hard pushed to deny.

" A few wee gins and tonics son", she laughed, " Down at the bingo with the girls on Saturday, rare fun too!"

"How much is a 'few' Agnes... we heard you were on a bottle a day!"

"Ooh, not every day", she replied, giggling.

I chipped in, "Was it the gin that caused the tumble Agnes?, thats's quite a bruise you've got there on your face".

She rubbed her face, gently as if still sensitive to the pain, "Aye, right-enough son, the coffee table broke my fall on the way down", she laughed again, but less so..

We laughed too, but politely, knowing the coffee table was innocent, her husband Jerry, was not.

Jerry saved the worst till Saturday, knowing Agnes would be out with the girls at bingo, where she would have 'a few' herself, some bought at the bar at the bingo club, some from out of the flask in her handbag.

Jerry was a hand-full, and difficult company being unemployed for many years, Agnes's income was enough for them to survive on whilst his drink-money came from the compensation fund Jerry had received from an industrial accident which occurred many years previously, and which, according to neighbours, was surely Jerry's own fault due to drinking on the job.

He had nothing to do, drink kept him occupied until the day a heart-attack took him out whilst he was sitting on the toilet, a rather small toilet in a small bathroom, and as such, difficult, especially with the rigormortis, to remove onto a stretcher after we got the official call for a police removal to the city mortuary.

Agnes never cried. Composed and meek at Jerry's funeral, she allowed herself to be fussed, bubbled-over and cried-on by her daughter Amber who was busy being seen to be upset at the funeral, and wailed audibly at the graveside, much to the priests annoyance as it disrupted his advice on the evils of abortion.

Many present for the service whispered that Amber was surprisingly troubled for a daughter who had never visited her parents in over two years, not even to show them her growing son, John-Anthony, for whom she had great ambition.

"He won't be like the scum from round here", she retorted to staff at the local kids nursery. "He is going to be a professional in life, and make his mum proper proud".

It seemed that little John-Anthony was not getting much say in the matter.

He wanted for nothing... except a visit to see his grandparents.

As soon as the funeral was by Amber was round to check on her mother.

"That bruise is healing up nice", she stated, unconcerned.

"Mum, you should probably use a bit more make-up to tone down the mark thats left".

"Yes dear", said Agnes.

"You will be too upset with the loss, so I will sort out the estate for you, seeing as I actually have a lawyer", she added, "A friend you know, does me special rates like I'm one of his family".

Agnes nodded her approval, her arms still folded.

Two weeks later, and without Amber's consent, Agnes handed in her notice and finished up as a cleaner in the hospital.

We had a whip-round for her and presented a signed card along with a shopping token for fifty pounds, 'from all her friendly undertaker pals' the card read.

"Call us if you need some company!" we added.

She laughed... she loved the banter.

"I will get me a summer dress with this", she said as we finished the sponge cake and tea provided by the hospital for the occasion.

"I fancy some sunshine to go with my freedom", she concluded knowingly, and then gave us all a hug.

When Amber found out that Agnes had sold her house, which Amber thought was still rented off the council, she was furious at the wilfull deception.

When Amber discovered via a letter received the following week, that Agnes has gone to Thailand to stay with 'friends' for a few months, she was livid.

The plan to have her mother put into a nursing home would have to be postponed.

When Amber discovered that her mother's bank account, containing all Jerry's left-over compensation money was transferred to another bank, and that the account she was aware of was closed, and that her joint-account application status had been therefore denied, she was positively raging!.

A few years later John-Anthony received a letter at the hostel he was then staying at containing a plane ticket to Thailand. He went immediately, and he never returned the Glasgow.

Amber never got to hear about this.

Agnes still drinks gin and tonics... but apparently a lot less than she used to.

Chapter Nine

Whisky Festivals and Whisky Clubs

Notes.
... a fully rounded and smoky cluster of sensation complexi-
ties. Some subtleties, some assertiveness, ends well.

I once tried to be an alcoholic quite by chance and with the opportunity presenting itself, however, I simply could not sustain the
commitment and dedication required for even modest success.

For me, being *really* drunk is not comfortable, simply not a
happy place at all.

One might find in the situation of functioning alcoholics, who
are individuals who may often present an outward facade of being
articulate, competent, even smart at times, but behind the facade of
the body which connects to the outside world there exists another
world where communication with others and oneself is selective,
restrained, and even heavily censored.

That's often the reality for the alcoholic, a circumstance which
most of us avoid, not by choice, but by personal modesty, lack of
addictivness vice, and our general situation in life.

Those unfortunate to become dependent on anti-depressants pre-
scribed by doctors often encounter the same situation.

We have to be so careful with most drugs where a little quantity
is medicinal, whilst too much can kill slowly, or less slowly.

Sure, there have been times when I unwittingly drank too much
whisky due primarily to the situations where I simply lost track of
volume.

One such occasion was a Whisky Festival held for the first time during 2001 in Edinburgh called 'Whisky Fringe' and located in an imposing, and stylish old public building called Mansfield Traquair, a Victorian Catholic Apostolic church completed in 1885 with a unique outstanding feature of having a large mural painted in the 1890s around the internal walls by a talented artist named Phoebe Anna Traquair who quite literally put angels into the architecture, and many of them too, creating what has since been discribed as the Sistine chapel of the North.

In tune with the changing times, a fresh 'spirit' was being appreciated by all those with the foresight to buy tickets and discover the several hundred options of whiskies and other liquors perched in bottles on tables lining the walls. Out of respect, the altar was carefully covered up and screened off from view so that no offence to religious types would be caused.

No offence appeared to be taken!

It was a bright but blustery day as I made my way from Partick in Glasgow, by train via Queen Street railway station, to Waverley station in Edinburgh. Along the line one gets a clear view at Linlithgow of the now redeveloped St Magdelene Distillery on the right hand side of the track as the train passes through the station heading eastwards. I felt a shiver along with a sudden sense of nostalgia for a whisky making place which I had not recognised on sight before, but now knew well from smelling and tasting numerous versions of the single malt over the last few years. It seemed such a waste that a successful distillery producing very characterful whisky should be simply shut down, stripped of its heart, its stills then removed, then converted into flats for commuters and first time buyers looking for a temporary place to live before becoming more ambitious for larger bedrooms in better 'locations'.

Many distilleries over the years have suffered this fate, none more tragic than Littlemill, Scotland's oldest distillery.

In Edinburgh, it was, of course, cold and a bit wet. Despite the colourful bustle and contrived cheer of the Edinburgh Arts' Festival in full swing, the tempering gusts of rain-strewn wind hurried me quickly along the pavements to a local pie shop called the PieMan for three hot pies of different fillings accompanied by a large cup of creamy coffee, which are the perfect companions for a whisky festival as they line the stomach and provide good personal anchorage before consuming possibly a bit too much than planned for... which from personal experience, is a real hazard and something to be wary of.

A mile's walk on cobbled streets took me to the door of Whisky Fringe and it was evident from the calibre of whisky-fan queued up outside of the front door awaiting entry that there were great expectations and connoisseurs were out in force today! The doors opened precisely on the intimated time, tickets were collected and we, the adoring malt-faithful, entered the church to worship at the altars of maltiness!

We were all spoiled for choice, not just by the range of what was official bottlings, presented on many of the tables, but also the much-welcomed presence of a good selection of independent bottlers, many of whom I had never seen at any of the Whisky Live shows in Glasgow.

Word soon spread throughout the hall amongst the hubub of coversations and chatter about some tables having 'extra drams under the covers'. Having just finished my fourth generous pour (about 15ml) from the fourth exhibitors table I took the chance of asking at the next table "do you have a wee special under the desk?", the response was immediate, and with a grin the presenter lifted out a fine old twenty five year old Clynelish and discreetly poured me a dram, it was pure nectar!

I was ecstatic.

"Thanks for that, much appreciated".I responded in genuine appreciation.

"No problem", was the reply from the affable ambassador. "At the next table they have some thirty year old Glenfarclas, but you best be quick my friend, as they are quickly running out".

I headed off, still clutching a glencairn glass of finest Indi-bottled Clynelish, and sought out the best access past the group of whisky fans now crowding the Glenfarclas table, in order to gain strategic advantage for another special dram.

Patience, as always, is a virtue, and requiring a calculated game-plan. Mine was to head round the back of a poster stand beside the venue wall and to shuffle sideways to the end of the targetted table then simply finish my dram and be seen to rinse the glass slowly with water obtained from a plastic bottle I got at the front door on arrival.

This protocol of rinsing is much appreciated by festival presenters as it indicates to them that you are removing all previous residual content from your glass, to freshen both glass and palate for another dram, and not simply looking for a fast top-up of 'whatever'.

I asked the question, carefully, politely, saying that the Glenfarclas thirty was 'recommended' by a 'friend in the Industry''. It worked, and I shuffled carefully back from the crowded table with a very decent dark tinged aromatic glass of finest old Speysider malt courtesy of Glenfarclas Distillery.

It was pure bliss! I couldn't rush it, swig it, gulp it, knock-it-back! I had to sip slow and savour over many minutes.

I looked at my whisky note book held in my other hand and felt inspired to add more tasting notes.

It's something I used to do then, but don't do now, but I'm glad I did it when I did it, which was to write down brief tasting notes at whisky festivals.

As well as disciplining the personal focus on identity of smell and taste, writing down notes shows a festival that one is a true and authentic 'anorak' and participating out of appreciation for the liquors rather than for just getting pished a bit more slowly at a classy venue whilst enjoying good stuff on the cheap.

It's a fact, a hard fact, that if one adds up the bar-retail value of all the liquors consumed at a reputable Festival like Whisky Fringe in Edinburgh, that one would pay ten times (or more) in a bar compared to a Whisky Fest. Also, experienced industry professionals are on hand to advise, inform, and help, and to this day I applaud the patience, perseverance and calm demeanour of all who stand sober behind Festival tables and pour for up to six hours at a time, dram after dram, retaining a calmness and sobriety whilst punters and attendees get less and less sober, whilst becoming more opinionated, more critical, more applauding, more disparaging, more loud-voiced, more interested, and some, more leery towards the products on display.

For practical reasons I have always been happier being an undertaker rather than the notion of being a whisky ambassador, having to deal with people when they are both sober and inebriated.

At least when one is an undertaker, any drunk people attending funerals are generally better behaved due to the gravity of the circumstances. Not so at a whisky event where the occasional arsehole who is bad enough when sober, will always be a lot worse when they are trying to get pished!

There was one occasion when I attended a whisky tasting event in an up-market shopping mall in Glasgow at short notice, after I received a phone call from a whisky club member who could not make it. I was assured that there would be 'phenomenal drams'.

I arrived to find a large table set up within the catering area of the mall, discreetly screened off with some bushy green potted plants and a disused escalator.

The atmosphere was all wrong! The presenter from Gordon and MacPhail Independent bottlers did his professional-best, but, of the fourteen of us seated at the table, one, and it only takes one, participant was an arsehole right from the start.

Question after question after question was fired at the brand ambassador who maintained a totally stoic demeanour throughout. After the third whisky, I apologised to the presenter, got up, and left. I had to, before I smashed an (empty) whisky bottle over the head of the self-indulgent, sneering, pompous little, rasin-faced prick who was continuing to ask more questions, stupid questions, simply, *attention seeking* questions... There were no phenomenal drams anyways!

I headed off to buy chocolate.

Back now to the Whisky Fringe in Edinburgh, where I notice to my surprise that after a couple of hours I have completed two pages in my notebook of tasting notes, each and every dram listed in chronological order and with any eccentricities highlighted. I don't bother counting as I feel perfectly sober, thanks to the pies I scoffed before arriving which provided a suitable lining for my stomach thus softening the ingress of alcohol.

Pacing of consumption is also a useful strategy for prolonging sobriety.

Moving systematically around the tables in an anti-clockwise direction I made a mental note of future festival protocols: -

- Eat plenty of carbohydrates before you arrive and never attend a whisky festival on an empty stomach.
- Never have any alcohol before you go to a festival, or drink significant quantities of alcohol the night before.
- Dress sensibly, with walking shoes for 100% comfort.
- Don't put on any perfume or after-shave lotions as they will interfere with the complex odours of whiskies and really piss-off other whisky fans.
- Have a shoulder bag to carry bottles of water in with which to refresh one's palate regularly. The festival should provide bottles of water and water urns for refilling your bottle.
- If a whisky is NOT good, don't waste precious time with it, pour it out your glass, rinse your glass with water... and start again. All Festivals should have spittoon buckets available.
- If a particular table is busy with attendees, find a quieter table for speedier attention and glass fill.

It is not necessarily the case that busy tables have better whisky, they may simply have more *fashionable* whisky, like a lack-lustre Port Ellen or fudgy old Brora.

- Start your event with unpeated whiskies with lighter flavours like Glenfiddich and Bladnoch as after a few peat-bomb whiskies like Ledaig and Laphroaig, your sense of taste will be shot to pieces by phenolic overload.

Peaty whiskies are best left till last, in the final hour of the event.

- Be open-minded, if there are rums, tequilas and bourbons on show, try them, you never know, if they're good, the quality will be self-evident in comparison to some malts or blends you may be experiencing.
- Back-off the tables in the last fifteen minutes of the Festival, don't join the desperados who rush the presenters for a "last wee goldy" and make a nuisance of themselves. I kid you not, I have actually seen presenters and ambassadors have to hold up the table they are standing behind to stop the crush of post-sober attendees charging forwards in the dying minutes of a festival desperate for one last fill, one last chug, one last swill of *anything*!

It is not a pretty sight to see.
Not nice at all.
Don't be part of it.

- Get home safely, DON'T go to the pub to drink more. DON'T stagger into the nearest liquor store for a bottle of cheaper malt just to 'kill the remains of the day'.
- Have a clear strategy for getting home being aware you are NOT sober. Have bus or train times noted down and a clear home-route strategy even if it means spending money on a taxi or arranging a nominated driver to pick you up. Drunk people in public places are vulnerable people, especially if well dressed and appearing to carry money... just sayin!.
- The following day, whilst still fresh in one's mind, take to Twitter, Facebook, e-mail etc and provide positive public feed-back to acknowledge a successful Whisky Festival.

One should make time to go directly to the organisers' and compliment them for a successful event and affirm how much, and why, you enjoyed it.

-       Any negative issues encountered at the event should be tactfully brought to the organizers' attention via a personal, verifiable message, usually by e-mail.

They should respond.

-       Finally, review what you have learned and establish what you have enjoyed. A particular brand of single malt, an unexpectedly tasty, less-sweet rum, a particularly helpful brand representative who it might be worth flagging-up to their employer as being a great ambassador for their Distillery.

What glass you used as provided by the Event, what prices they were charging for their products at tables, what interesting chats you had with fellow event maltsters and malt-mates.

A good Whisky Festival is worth its weight in single cask malt!

I conclude this little story of my inaugural Whisky Fringe Festival in Edinburgh which was the first of many I attended and all very good quality events managed with enthusiasm and professionalism, with a timely tale of amnesia.

This situation happened to me only once, and has never happened again. I learned!

I woke up in bed the morning after the day before with the details of the Festival already receeding in my conscious mind and blearily examined my bed-side table alarm clock. It said ten a.m.

All good, I thought, glad I had all of Sunday to recover.

I drank lots of water from the pint glass on standby beside the clock and got up for wash, a pee, and a cup of tea.

Downstairs in the kitchen I was shocked to see neatly sitting on the table, an empty plate, knife, fork and napkin, all there, except for the dinner I had cooked myself on returning home from Edinburgh. I was confused.

I carefully examined first the plate then the cooker to piece together the meal of fried beef steak, oven chips, green peas, diced carrots, mayonnaise and horseradish sauce.

I had no recollection whatsoever of having made and eaten this meal the night before.

My mind was a blank.

I turned to my whisky notes book still lying in the shoulder bag left inside the front door. Sure enough, forty five tasting notes, including smells, tastes and finishes of forty five drams consumed at the Festival.

That was, on calculation, forty five times, ten millilitres, or more, which equals four hundred and fifty millilitres or .45 of a litre of mainly cask strength assorted liquors consumed over a five hour period. Very little had been discarded at the event!.

I made a mental note to be a little more cautious with my enthusiasm for all subsequent whisky festivals.

This is the thing about experience in life, it's about having the *experience* to learn from that experience. It is at the margins of our limits that we identify our limits and learn to manage them for the sake of our longevity and health.

I now look back on these early and very committed days of yester-year at just how much consistency over time I put into smelling, tasting and appreciating whiskies and other quality liquors. I reflect now on how, over time, I have evolved sensibility and eased-off on the poorer quality I used to tolerate, along with appreciating the better quality that I know now with more familiarity, accompanied by restraint. It's skill that comes with experience.

Still, back in the heady and bustling days of the early and mid 2000's I can now see in retrospect that I had a good 'run', particularly with Glasgows Whisky Club, where I learned a lot, not just from the people who attended the malt-moments, but also from the tremendous variety of whiskies smelled, tasted, mulled-over and contemplated by all present at these meetings.

One such later-on, club moment around 2009, saw the usual

gang of around thirty members seated around several tables in the club venue, the Bon Accord in North Street, Charing Cross where Paul the proprietor showed quite an interest in our gatherings and frequently joined in with the chats.

He confided in us that he was looking to expand his whiskies and cask-ale selection further and host other whisky-related events at the bar. He would often solicit recommendations, opinions and gossip from club-goers and he eventually concluded that he should start a Bon Accord whisky club of his own, and have it meet on a different night.

We all knew each other quite well at this point, and as you well know malt-mates, whisky is a great ice-breaker between relative strangers. We were all, after about six or so years now, well past the point of being strangers, we were in fact, if not quite buddy-friends, then affable company in an ambient environment of mutual appreciation and support for all stuff liquor-related.

Thirty members at a time seemed like a good limit for the club. At this point, there's enough people to get thirty decent measures from just one bottle. Also, enough faces without there being too many to try to put a name to, and get to know, without obvious cliques appearing. Sure, some got on better with each other than others, but at this stage there was no 'arsehole' involved to dampen the mood with their self-imposing ignorance and trollish behaviour. That happened after I had left the Club in 2010.

Bill Macintosh, as always, was in his capacity as Chairperson, and had protocols well under control, with everything being organised in advance and members advised to eat a good meal beforehand, and to observe their personal limits of consumption during the evening.

Initially, some Club nights had a 'bottles on the barrel' system where attendees were invited to take their club glencairn glass, and go to a conveniently positioned upturned hogshead cask, now used as bar furniture, where an assortment of around twenty bottles were placed as bought with club funds, or provided by distilleries and independent bottlers for samples.

Even at this time, whisky clubs of some visibility were seen by the Industry as having clout and influence on the sales of brands.

Although starting out with good intentions, inevitably a few club members would get a bit too greedy, fueled by previous good-times into consuming a bit and a bit and a bit more... more than was 'good'.

After one boisterous night, it was decided to limit the availability of volume of bottles on the barrel. I think Bill, for logistical reasons, preferred evenings where a brand ambassador in their capacity as a brand communicator would appear from a Distillery and share a few of their range, during which feed-back was sought, and generally appreciated.

One memorable ambassador, on this occasion from an Indi bottler called Duncan Taylor who used to bottle some good stuff, especially scotch grain whisky like Carsbridge.

She was called Jacqueline Sutherland and she looked like a youngish, cheery librarian who would not mind book-readers making a bit of noise, if it meant they read books properly. Being dressed entirely in a quality, co-ordinated pink tweed outfit with shiny brogues added to her character.

Not fashionable, but very stylish.

She held her tasting evening at the OranMor Bar in the west end of the City at the top of Byres Road. On arriving late she declared herself to be 'starving' and ate two bananas while we waited patiently for the show to start.

Thereafter, on finishing the two bananas, she went on to state that she did not know much about whisky really, but would appreciate our thoughts. The night was excellent, one of the best the Club had. No routine pre-rehearsed scripts, no flannel, no caramel-coated poor quality whiskies being touted as *great expressions* in the *category'*, no industry attitude and the, we-know-best-so-there conceit, no, none of that, Jacqueline was fabulous as a host!

The whiskies were all excellent too, and some older stuff was in the glasses, eccentric stuff individual stuff, *less-obvious* stuff and just perfect for the experienced palates of all those gathered for the night.

The venue itself was very characterful, lots of Scottish baronial ambiance, muted traditional lighting, quality heavy dark-wooden furnishings. The attendees were the main-stay of the club, Bill, Juliette, Bobby Banford, Jarkko, Stefan, Andy Bell, and myself amongst others.

A new club member joined us called Tam Gardner. Looking like someone who had just received a sudden electric shock, and fond of dressing in black, he was an inquisitive whisky fan who had ambitions to open his own whisky shop in the west end of the city as he speculated that interest and demand would be growing further for malt-stuff, especially peated and sherried malt-stuff.

Most of use just laughed at the concept of prices increasing much further, after all, bottles were expensive enough as it was and we were all getting more budget-concious and aware of our spending limits.

It was one of these nights where everything just comes together after an inauspicious start and the mellow malt-magic weaves its constant subtle spell infusing the good, and worthy company assembled with a perfect positive ambiance and accord of good-will, shared excellence, and unstated philosophy of all that's best about being human.

It really does not get much better.

It takes a lot more than whiskies to make a good whisky-night, whether by solo or with others, all good whisky meetings need to silently summon an ethereal angel for company who's presence endorses all assembled, and enriches the moment through that blessing with a little magic, which causes such good humour and atmosphere, that the moment is hard to forget even after many years dulled by life's habit for forgetfulness.

Don't get me wrong, good whiskies help, in fact they are important for the occasion, and with poor quality whiskies the mood of the moment can quickly become spoiled. However, there is no doubt in my mind that such is the narcotic influence of alcohol sipped slowly, a positive-charged atmosphere freed from all negative elements therein will elevate the experience to sublime and devine.

Bad whiskies in bad company, as I'm sure you will appreciate, have the very opposite effect.

I won't bore you with those details.

A 'brand ambassador' has a horrible job where the whisky tasting location is 'wrong' for the event, the whiskies poor and flat, with poor quality cask influence, chill filtration and added colourant with the branding pretentious, disingenuous and misleading. Then to round all that off, a selfish, indifferent, and possibly antagonistic crowd who don't care for anything except getting more liquor and getting more tipsy... ideally for free, with expected 'gifts' at the end of the presentation.

I would miss these halcyon moments created in the past, however the experience of them allows me to prepare for the present, and plan for the future, based of the experience of these events.

The Club is back in the Bon Accord again, for another 'roll of the barrel' so to speak, but this time it's oddly different. The brand ambassador appears confident and authoritative, the whiskies are fine, but what has changed is the club itself, it has moved-on, grown-up, matured and has greater expectation along with standards of what is valid and invalid about whisky.

We are being stuck with yesterday's messages on today's notice-board, and the Industry has not noticed.

Half way though the pedestrian presentation which is too slow, too detailed, too dull, and there are too many pauses between drams, Juliette who is, as usual, sitting next to me, turns round discreetly and quietly whispers.

"You should be hosting this event, it would be more informative and more fun", she states with some authority of her own based, no doubt, on experience of our chats and banters.

I agree, I could do better!

It's the following week and I am in Saint Andrews, a medieval up-market University town in the Kingdom of Fife. It's November and dry with a biting cold wind billowing up the grass and dunes around the local golf courses.

Whilst out walking around the town with my long-aquainted friends Stevie and Jaquie, and playing with their two young sons Harry and Charlie, who are showing me manoeuvers on their scooters, I accidently trip over the top of one of the small flimsy scooters whilst foolishly attempting to impress the kids by riding the vehicle down a concrete slope into a sand dune.

I fail miserably and head-dive right over the top of the scooter in a slow-motion fashion that looks quite entertaining, but results in a sudden shock of pain throughout my right shoulder as I face-plant into the sand.

It's a disaster, I have sprung my clavicle where it articulates to my collar bone and shoulder joint, and spend the next four hours in the outpatients department of the local hospital.

I stay the night with my friends and they console me in my misfortune, Harry and Charlie think it's hilarious at first, but then they too offer some genuine sympathy and affable encouragement.

I am signed off work for two months and cannot carry coffins or lift stuff.

This is the first time in my life that I have been off sick for more than a few days and as soon as the pain subsides from the injury I go stir-crazy around my house in need for something to do, anything except drink whisky to alleviate the pain!

My little brother Clive phones eventually to console and motivate me into being a bit more positive under the circumstances and also to suggest a few things I might do with the sudden extra time on my hands.

I say 'little' brother but in fact he is about six inches taller than me and about twelve inches wider so he is in fact a 'bigger' little brother, one whom I stopped hitting many years ago, which is normally one of the most important duties of being a bigger brother, until one gets too small and gets hit back. He is actually quite sincere in his sympathies which is not what I expect, and makes a few flippant suggestions as to what I can do, or might do, to pass the time as my shoulder heals.

"How about you go online and do a blog?" he suggests, mumbling down the phone in a slightly bored, half-interested voice.

"Get a camera and do a video of your motorbike or garden" he drawls.

"I might visit if I get time, but probably not actually".

I thank him and hang up, making a mental note to call him back in two days with feedback on the 'incredibly exciting' thing I'm doing.

It's a Glasgows whisky club night again, and I'm looking forward to seeing what's the 'bottles on the barrel' options. Juliette is in contemplative mood chatting to Club-regular Mark Connolly who has set up a whisky forum called whiskywhiskywhisky.com where spirit-fans can chat to one another freely, without the dogmatic degree of censorship applied at some other forums.

His site has filled a hole within the online whisky community and his subscribers are growing rapidly.

Juliette is hearing all about it.

I mention that my brother is suggesting I do a blog, to which both Juliette and Mark nod in agreement that it is a rather good idea, and that I should do it.

The following morning, after a hefty session the night before, I get stuck into my first blog post at ralfy.com, linked to the Google blogspot option which works and is free.

I get five 'hits' on my first day.

Success.

After about six more carefully worded and entertaining posts that get a lack-lustre response I pull the plug on it. The first blog attempt is over, it was fun, but it had no *traction*.

I phone Clive for advice, but he's not interested.

"If it was easy" he declares, "everybody would do it, and anyways... you're nothing special".

I watch a movie instead, something about pirates and treasure.

It is while I am doing some movie fact-checks on line, that I decide that the YouTube video format might be worth a look-see, to find out what whisky reviews are like as a video rather than a written blog.

Single Malt TV seem to have the best conventional content, and a good assortment of videos covering a wide variety of subjects relating to Scotch, otherwise it appears to be a few, mainly American, commentators sitting in front of a computer screen live-commenting their brief opinions on several standard liquors.

They don't seem to have much in the way of a growing audience.

I pretend to be doing the same as they are, but in my own space, and minus a computer screen.

Not sure if it's working or would appeal to people, however I reckon I have a good accent for the role of online whisky commentator.

Time, as they say... will tell.

Chapter Ten

More Vlogs and Blogs and Stuff

Notes.
.... dank and dusty aromas of yester-year waft around enouraging us to ignore marketing hype and get ourselves more informed...

Something I think you need to know malt-mates, and it only becomes apparent after some years of experience, smelling and tasting a lot of varieties of whiskies on a regular basis.

The collective experience of enjoying whisky is governed to a certain extent by the law of diminishing returns.

In other words, as time goes on we all get a bit more fussy, and begin to find faults in whiskies where we never noticed them before due to our inexperience, but as we are more experienced now, and will gain further experience in the future, so one of the little tricks is to enjoy a dram entirely on its own merits whatever age it is or however available or basic it may be.

The risk we all face is that after a while, in fact a few years is all it may take, is that we become blasé about whiskies and increasingly closed-minded as to what consitutes quality and what deserves our attention and money, then we get bored!

We should be on our guard against becoming insitutionalised in our whisky interests where we become part of the scene purely by default, and end up in the company of others where there's a lot of mutual back-slapping over Islay peating-levels, 1970s Arbegs, what constitues a 'sherry monster' and who is the most boring master blender in the Business!

… Yyyyyyyyawn!

We all need to keep things fresh in our perspectives and opinion even though the spirits industry is all about very similar, usually pedestrian 'initiatives', designed to add innovation to the 'category'.

I know they are constrained by legislation which is heavy-handed on alcohol, however the frequently condescending official scripts within some distilleries are driven by superficial commercial convenience and not by a genuine long-term interest in the customer.

Managers who make more profit through cutting production costs for a Company are usually well rewarded, despite the longer-term consequences which can sometimes cause bigger, unforseen costs by impact and loss of sales, it has happened before and it will happen again.

You will find that if you get too close to the 'scene' you get caught up in it, then risk losing your objective focus on simply enjoying a few drams of good quality liquor in your own space, and in your own time.

When involved in the wider scene socially you risk getting distracted by malt-politics, who's who, and what's where, and when's whatever!

Brand ambassadors become 'personality' show-people, and if they are lucky, get something consistently decent to present for appreciation to selective consumers with few grumbles or negative feed-back.

Master blenders can get elevated to celebrity status by a small minority of fans who want to get bragging rights in the maltosphere of social medias, exercising largesse, influence, opinion and status over whoever subscribes and participates into the *theatre*.

It just the way it is, it's real life, it's human nature.

I think it's better to view things from a distance and focus on really enjoying the smell and taste sensations of any decent spirit you can find, and even better, find at value for money, and without too much fuss.

I'm not trying to be all hardcore about this by suggesting you take this journey in complete isolation, but rather, that you keep focus on the real reason for your interest in spirits, and occasionally connect with an event or group of like-minded souls for the purposes of maltertainment.

Just don't dive into the local whisky scene too deep.

… just sayin'!

The iritation of my shoulder injury has now subsided and the pain is gone leaving a stiffness and mild ache.

When I tripped over the scooter in St Andrews it was one of the worst injuries of my life and only a little less painful than when I picked up a nasty ear infection diving in the Panama canal as part of a marine archeological survey in the early 1980s, that was the worst pain ever!

With a note from my doctor keeping me off my employment for two months, I was rapidly getting stir-crazy around the house, and even the more frequent walks through the west end of Glasgow were not filling enough time in the day.

I needed another thing to do.

My little brother Clive had already suggested I do something on the internet, as it was getting more popular as a medium for communication, so one wet and miserable morning mid-week I had started to write a whisky blog on the Google 'blogger' template. I had tried it but it did not work.

Brother Clive had sent me a link to a new electronic device just made available on Amazon.

It was called a Flip Cam UltraHD.

I looked at the online specs and glowing reviews, thought about it, bought it, loved it.

The Flip HD Cam is the perfect product at the right time, 2009, the interenet being only about twenty years old by then and still in its infancy. youtube.com, the internet's most prominent video-based provider had been only around for about four years.

The first ever video posted on YouTube was on the 23rd April 2005 and called 'Me At The Zoo', it has now exceeded sixty-six million views by 2019.

After only four years of self-creator videos, quality is quite patchy, and content a bit home-spun, but I immediatly noticed that video content relating to whisky is more informed and simply more interesting than the bland, but superficial content that is available on television.

Quite simply, television, especially the BBC programmes realating to spirits, wine, or beer, are presented in a condescending, traditionalist, conservative and fake way. There was one particularly dull and self-indulgent BBC programme called 'Oz and James drink to Britain', which was simply a couple of self-indulgent, boring oafs talking crap and getting pissed with occasional flippant opinion on wines.

The whole programme reeked of snobbery, self-indulgence and conceit... in my opinion!

I never watch television now, I have not done for five years.

I don't pay my BBC licence fee, I don't have to as I don't connect with the BBC in any way.

I unplugged!

It improved my quality of life dramatically when I did so.

More time to spend on better stuff.

More time for me in the real World.

Some online content is not much better than the TV rubbish, however to its credit, at least it's genuine, original, and often entertaining.

I think I could do better, provide more accurate content, give beter opinion, after all, I had experience, the accent, the contacts... the time-served 'apprenticeship'.

I bought a tripod, a couple of spot-lighters and set up the Flip Cam UltraHD to record.

The UltraHD is a small, cigarette packet sized plastic and aluminium unit of sturdy construction in which two standard AA batteries are placed for power. Everything is automatic, focus, exposure, image management etc There's an on/off button on the side of the unit, three buttons on the back, two smaller 'play' and 'delete' buttons, and in the centre, a larger red 'record' button. Above is a small, clear screen to show what is recording and on the other side of the on/off button is a slide-switch which releases a small contained arm which flips upwards and out revealing a USB plug.

It's simple, cheap, and very effective for internet recording in 2009.

We are still in the age of 'dial-up' connections.

Sitting at a table in the house near the window, for some extra light, I stare at the passive lens of the camera. Nothing happens.

I breathed deeply to marshall my thoughts... what to say, . . what to review... what to mention and not mention.

It is cold, still in winter, and a sudden shiver sends me out of the room for a warmer jacket, and whilst I am at it, a tweed bunnet to wear on my head. I look in the hall mirror and laugh at myself, just a typical Scottish 'bloke' in a country pub enjoying a dram and a beer.

Returning to the table with the camera all set up and ready to record, I grab a bottle of Canadian Glen Breton ten year old single malt, sitting on a near-by shelf, that would do for practice.

Tasting unusual, compared to Scotch, this bottle is much in my mind as the Scotch Whisky Associaton has spend millions trying to get this distillery to remove the word 'Glen' from it's branding as it could suposedly cause confusion with Scotch whiskies identity.

I did not agree with this opinion. A distillery called Glen Ora in Nova Scotia, Canada and lying sixty miles south of Inverness, Nova Scotia, can, in my opinion, call itself whatever 'Glen' it wants to.

That is simply an indigenous Scottish cultural perspective. Not a corporate commercial one.

I'm sitting at the table with a few props along with the Glen Breton, a strip of oak wood to hide my notes and a few other bottles of assorted malty-stuff scattered around, some are in view, and some out of view of the camera. I stare at the camera until I realise that it won't switch itself on to record, I need to do that, and it does not have a remote button.

I get up from the seat, walk round the table and press the red button. A red 'recording' light appears in the casing on the front of the camera beside the lens.

I scurry back round to the seat and stare a bit more at the camera.

"Hello, and err, this video is err! Ummm! Aaaaah! A review of scotch whisky, ooops!"

I dive round the table and turn off the recording.

First blooper, first discarded video... one of a few over the years.

I pause before pressing 'record' again and slow up my return to the seat.

"Hello Malt fans and welcome to this first whisky review and my whisky today is Glen Brighton!"

Second Blooper.

I take a few deep breaths and consider how I might have a slower start to the videos in order to allow myself more time to think about what I am about to say next, before I say it!

"Hello malt fans".

"Greeting whisky mates".

"Well, hello mates of maltiness".

"How are you then malts and mates".

I then give up on the idea as impractical and just start the video, the fifth take with -

"Hello there, Ralfy here and welcome to my three minute whisky review".

For three minutes and seventeen seconds I chat calmly about what I have in the glass from the bottle.

At the end, I put the kettle on for a cup of tea and look over the recording.

I reckon it's good enough to go public.

It goes public, but not until I have recorded a second whisky review about Talisker ten year old single malt entitled 'Whisky Review 1 – Talisker 10yo' which gets released first as I think a well known scotch whisky will get a better response than an obscure Canadian malt.

After a few phone calls to whisky friends and my first hour 'live' on YouTube, I get my first hundred 'hits'. I am delighted, there are no negative comments. Yet!

By the time I start to record the third review there are no out-takes or discarded attempts, it all comes together in one single take. No editing, no background music, no fancy stuff, so the one-take 'winging-it' style of video blog including mistakes, bloopers and trip-ups which all stay in the final presentation. This is a formula which has worked for me in such a positive way that I have never changed the style, it has simply become part of my persona.

Whisky review three is a popular Aberlour cask strength version, attracting some interest in whisky circles due to the price and good quality, then four, five, six vlogs, then the first troll arrives, and criticizes me in their blogs.

The sporadic negativity and hissy-fits are the best thing to happen, suddenly I'm relevent to the whisky scene!

I get noticed.

One such hisser states in his blog about me - 'self-important whisky nerd with a tripod in his face', which is actually perfectly true, and I am flattered even though I am not supposed to be flattered.

My malt-mate, Mark Connelly at Glasgows Whisky Club rushes to my defence online, bless 'im, and suddenly it's a conversation thread at the prominent whisky forum whiskywhiskywhisky.com where the buzz, and resulting publicity gets my viewing figures soaring.

I've arrived!

Flawed, irratic, opinionated, eccentric, all these things are true, and the audience seem to love it!

I'm sitting with the Glasgows Whisky Club crowd on a Tuesday night in the Bon Accord, and publican Paul wanders over before the malt-moments start to congratulate me on getting the vlogs up and running. Chairman Bill is not so pleased for some reason, which I think is due to his newspaper-editor instincts of realising that online content means less reason for people to buy newspapers.

He's right of course.

"It will just be a flash in the pan", he spits, uncharacteristically.

Juliette who is sitting next to me is far more positive.

"Well done, keep it up, with your knowledge you might have a few more years ahead of you with this".

I thank her kindly, I appreciate the support.

Even the usually affably-cynical and very measured Bobby Banford has a good word to say.

We have another excellent evening of assorted whiskies and after a bit of a break the following day, I sit down again to record another review.

There's an e-mail for me! A big Distillery want to send me a bottle of whisky to review.

I think about it for a minute or two and then come to the conclusion that with all the stock of bottles I have, I will just do it myself, without endorsement, after all, free stuff is an unwritten contract, a 'bind'.

The beauty of the internet at this point of time is that it is still a young experience for many so it makes sense to try out the strategy of being independent in what I choose to review.

Once I accept 'free stuff' and Industry flattery, my perspective is no longer really my own.

Fine for television and advertising, people expect that the truth is not being told, these mediums are not about my sort of thing, so my game-plan morphs naturally, I will be everything NOT found on T.V., no editing, no glamerous suroundings, no smoozing over certain brands who might pay me the most. I leave that to others.

Then the Industry invites arrive,

this 'event',

that 'launch',

then the 'private party',

then the 'checking out' for suitablity as a potential ambassador for a brand.

Importantly, the professionals want to see as soon as possible whether any on-line proactive 'influencers' attending such events can be modest in their consumption and not get pished, loud, gobby and disruptive!

Whisky Industry professionals, brand ambassadors and paid 'personalities' must always remain sober at all times... even when they are not!

Enthusiastic amateurs need more vigilance by the professionals when on location at events, as arsehole-behaviour can quickly blow-up online and impact reputations. The Industry must always be on its guard.

I politely decline invitations to events at first, but as the invites continue to filter through and make me increasingly nervous, I have no choice but to vlog publicly that I do not want to be contacted by marketing people.

If I want to, I will be in touch with them.

To their credit, the Industry generally adhere to this request and continue to do so over the following years.

It has made my situation a lot simpler, more refreshing, more transparent and less compromised.

It is acknowledged and appreciated.

I can totally understand that marketing departments want to engage with onliners who routinely get a bigger independent audience than most orthodox initiatives, and after all, marketeers just don't need onliners putting-down their products whether for quality, personal or ethical reasons.

For the money, humouring onliners is cheaper than traditional advertising where one full colour ad in a whisky magazine may cost upwards of four thousand pounds a page, per issue.

An official bottle, or even more convenient to them, a sample in a miniature bottle with a plain white label penned with a descriptor will probably be enough for an enthusiastic onliner to feel valued.

Don't get me wrong, marketing professionals really need to keep an eye online to become aware, as soon as possible, where and when their products may be getting complimented, criticized, or worse, totally misrepresented. One small *disclosure* left unaddressed for too long can gain traction online and become established as default fact. Not all bad comment is good publicity.

As briefly mentioned, I have been more than happy with the commercial maturity of the Scotch Whisky Industry not pestering me to publicise, promote, endorse or engage with their products or with the wider whisky scenes. I'm simply not team-spirited for such things.

I just stick to reviewing what I buy in shops, from bottles taken down off of shelves, which in my opinion more accurately represents what people are buying and drinking generally.

The wee undisclosed problem with pre-designated samples and batches in standard bottles sourced from marketeers is that they might, and I do mean 'might', not accurately represent what is being sold later to customers as standard product, but may be 'tasty' promotional versions which will help persuade promoters and journalists, and whisky on-liners, as to how great a specific whisky is in terms of smell and taste.

Such versions also may help sway judgement at Industry competitions... in my opinion!

Early on, to help control the number of bottles of whisky I was opening at any one time, I extended the range of my reviews to cover subjects like glassware options and visits to specialist retailers and distilleries.

The video recording at Loch Fyne Whiskies, whisky review 31, at Inveraray in the beginning of March of 2009 was a laugh.

As a regular customer of many years now, I knew the team well enough to approach Richard Joynson the proprietor to get permission to record something... anything. I had no idea what to record, but I now had enough self-confidence to let the recording take its course and see what evolved.

It would be useless to keep the recording static and pre-scripted which would have looked over-rehearsed and boring. As said before, it was self-evident that to be the risky, flawed, home-spun antithesis of traditional television was important and the less I tried to copy the BBC orthodoxy, the better for the originality and authenticity.

The consummate production-value failure of the video was part of its success.

It is cold and blustery when I arrived at the shop, a small, squat cottage concluding a neat photogenic line of shops terraced along Inverary's main street.

Laura and Andy are as always, immediately welcoming and friendly whilst Richard lurks behind his desk pressing buttons on his computer, one finger at a time. All is normal.

After the up-to-date chatter and compliments with Andy and Laura, I turn my attention to Richard who is still hiding behind his desk.

He is both amused and curious at my request and asks if it's going to take long as he has a bus-load of tourists arriving in fifteen minutes.

I reassure him that it will be one-take, no editing and nothing scripted except for a simple list of content.

Still amused and beginning to look a bit mischevous, Richard agrees to the recording taking place, so we begin.

The Flip HD Cam is attached to my tripod and I immediately get a few odd looks from the team at how insubstantial my studio equipment is. I ignore the looks and start recording, panning slowly along the glass cabinet filled with miniatures of assorted whiskies, quite a lot of mini bottles actually, which is the reason for the opening 'shot'.

Thereafter I pivot the camera round the walls of the shop taking in hundreds of bottles of whiskies until I come to a stop at the till desk where purchases are paid for, wrapped and claimed.

Richard looks nonchalantly at his shelves pretending to ignore the camera until I prompt him by breaking the silence with a, "Hello malt-moments, Ralfy here from ralfy.com".

This is really the moment when I decide to open every subsequent video thereafter with a *malt-mention*. It becomes a part of the experience.

I warble on with introducing Loch Fyne Whiskies as arguably the best whisky shop in the World as Richard decides to troll the recording by turning up the background music slightly too loud followed by creating 'rabbit ears' behind my head to entertain the viewers.

I don't of course notice this till after, but I don't care... it's entertaining and unscripted and real!

I continue on, "And somewhere here is Richard who owns the place and has a very good knowledge about whisky! ".

Richard shakes my hand and acting his part perfectly feigns

some alarm when I prompt him to disclose 'three hot tips' for en-joying whisky.

He joins in with "Ask me a question!", to which I prompt, "How's business?"

"Booming", he replys, then stalls!

I am having to work to maintain the 'flow' of this recording so I further prompt him with advice on selecting a flavour profile of whisky, smoky, fruity, peaty etc.

He gives some practical advice whilst fumbling around in his pocket with one hand... which looks a little bit awkward until I real-ise that he's actually quite nervous now the camera is recording.

He brings across a bottle of Inverarity Islay malt which repre-sents good value for money and has seen, judging by the fill-level, quite a lot of pours since opened.

I'm poured a glass and then he puts the bottle back on it's shelf whilst I immediately identify as a Speysider called Linkwood... ooops! My mistake, brilliant video!

"That's Islay whisky", points out Richard, whilst I rapidly be-come aware of my blatant blooper.

"There we are, that's 'live' for you", I retort with confidence.

"Were' doin;' fine folks, were' doin' fine!", I adlib.

"And your three tips for whisky?", I ask.

"Don't drop it!, Look forward to it!... and spend as much as you can in Loch Fyne Whiskies!" I ask him jokingly if that was not just a gratuitous plug for his shop at which point he immediately changes the subject onto whether I have tried the Loch Fyne Whisky liqueur yet.

I confirm that I have and add that it goes very well 50/50 with cask strength Laphroaig.

Richard leans to the camera and states, "busty nail", which is the name he has given the concoction.

We then conclude the recording amicably as Laura hovers into the frame to attend to a customer.

I can hear the approaching footsteps of a bus tour party and just before they enter the shop and as I whisk the tripod and camera out of the way, Richard adds, "You're not actually going to put that online? Are you!"

"Yes", I reply, "that was excellent Richard, the BBC would never dream of putting this on air, it will work a treat".

I conclude the moment.

"Bye everyone, thanks again", and then I hold the door open to allow about twenty slightly damp over-dressed tourists to shuffle into this Aladdins cave of maltiness.

It's now a year later and many malt-moment vlogs having been now recorded in Glasgow, and with a growing diverse audience I arrive at my last ever recording made in September 2010 on location whilst still living in Glasgow.

It's Whisky Review 177, and a series of about seven recordings made on location at Springbank Distillery Campbeltown, Scotland's most iconic and important single malt Distillery.

Springbank ambassador Peter Currie is the host, and a thoroughly decent guy too.

Every inch the sturdy Scotsman he has traces of a viking about his demeanour and exhibits an affable maturity for his relatively young age.

The thing about Springbank is simply that every stage in the production process takes place at the Distillery itself, and not only does it have this provenance, but also Springbank distillery is a labour intensive commercial operation which means vital, quality jobs are provided for the local community, a community that needs each and every job it can get.

It's that kind of community.

I was a late-comer to Springbank having tried many malts before, for whatever reason, eventually getting around to buying a bottle of the ten year old 'Springy'.

I think it is probably because there's not a lot made in the first place in terms of volume with Springbank being a small operation in the general scheme of all things malty, a fact further compounded by the situation where this small distillery is making three different versions of itself with the standard two-and-a-half-times (approximately) distilled Springbank, the double distilled and peaty Longrow, and the triple distilled Hazelburn. All are good!

The general publicity around Springbank is what one could realistically call 'low key' with virtually no advertising or brand ambassador embellishment, and certainly no pushy marketing teams firing off flannel to media.

As soon as I tasted the stuff, I liked it, all three versions of it. The reason was obvious really, unlike so many larger and more visible malt brands which are cosmetically coloured with industrial caramel, then chill-filltered, then diluted to 40% volume ethanol for 'consumer access', this little gem of a distillery always bottles higher strength and more naturally, always at least 46%vol: which in terms of intrinsic quality of smell and taste reward makes a huge difference to the customer in the experience of the product. Simple as that.

To compound this situation, production is what one would call old fashioned and un-modernised to be made 'accessible' for 'category consumer expectations', a situation that one often finds in some other less exciting malt brands.

The wage bill at Springbank must be high as distilleries go, however employment is the most effective way a business can return wealth generated by commerce back into the local community where it's made.

If ALL distilleries in Scotland operated on the same principles as Springbank, Scotland would have less unemployment and more communal wealth... simples!

"So", says Peter, "Welcome to Springbank, what are you looking to do?"

"Just wander round the Distillery from start to finish and record what happens", I propose.

Peter looks a little disconcerted, and it is clear that he was expecting more of a 'traditional' style of video recording with real cameras. He looks at my very modest Flip HD Cam stuck onto the end of the cheap tripod, and does not look any more reassured!

"Will that actually work when we go inside?" he quips, "It gets quite dark in the kilning area".

I give him a wink, "Well, tell you what, lets record the first ten minute 'bit' at the malting floors then I will play it back to you and you can see for yourself".

We proceed and I press the red button on the Flip... "Hello malty malt-floors", I chime, and then we're up and running and just under ten minutes passes in a flash as we spontaniously interact followed by a concluding, "Join us shortly... excellent", then off goes the red button.

"Well?" I ask as I play back the recording to Peter, "That's actually better than I expected", he remarks surprised at how easy the whole thing is turning out to be. We proceed with six more videos providing what at the time was the most comprehensive walk-through of any distillery to be found on the internet.

As we conclude in the Cadenheads tasting room attached to the Distillery, Peter confides that he had reservations about the potential publicity, but is now a lot calmer about it.

I remind him that if there's any problems with content I will remove the video, or any legitinmate complaints from online users and viewers, then I would recognise that and respond to the complaint. I don't expect any issues, there are, in fact, none.

On releasing the series of seven videos, one by one on You-Tube, response is very positive and affirming with many malt-mates getting their first view of this fascinating place for themselves.

Springbank is open to visitors and offers tours, and has an educational whisky-school however it is a bit remote compared to many other distilleries in Scotland, but the drive there is beautiful and worth the loch, sea, and ocean views if the day is calm and clear.

I get back home to Glasgow late that night. The three hour winding drive back along highland roads has been hassle-free in the general scheme of things, but, sitting in my kitchen with a fresh cup of tea, and a couple of bottles of Springbank purchased whilst at the Distillery, I feel weird.

I know the reason for this, I am in fact leaving my home in Glasgow for the last time tomorrow and it will thereafter become someone else's property.

After nearly thirty years living and working in the City I have to move to the Isle Of Man, a small, but busy island in the middle of the Irish Sea, and look after my dear old mother who now has advancing symptoms of dementia and can no longer look after herself.

She needs me now, and I won't be letting her down.

My whisky collection moves with me, of course, but it is self-evident that I will be needing a new place to record my whisky reviews. At the point of moving over on the ferry, I haven't a clue what I'm going to do about that.

Chapter Eleven
Finding the Whisky Bothy

Notes.

... a satisfying finish and conclusion of a precious malt-moment. Time and patience reveal hidden depths and less-familar flavours with expected nostalgia for tomorrow's drams.

I have just moved from Scotland westwards across the Irish Sea to the Isle of Man, twenty windy, and watery miles south of the Mull of Galloway, Scotland, it is a near-far-away place with sentimental attachment to my younger life.

As a child, we had family holidays every year to the island where we stayed for ten days at my grandparents house at a hilly and sprawling coastal village called Laxey. I don't remember much about my grandparents as they were both introverts, and our family visit was tolerated more than appreciated.

Perhaps it was having me and my brother around with all our naive excitement about summer, sea, sand and ice-creams and being visibly happy too, perhaps that's what disturbed them.

Even now, all these years later I look back with a constantly evolving nostalgia for these sun-drenched nautical days, where the island itself cast an instinctive and elemental spell over my child-hood providing an anchor of story-book retreat, away from the grind of growing up in a wet miserable town in Scotland, where I had no choice but to attend two concrete, bleachy, soulless schools intent on killing creativity, and withholding knowledge through the

National Curriculum of education.

I hated school, really, really, hated it from the moment I arrived at primary school to the moment I left secondary school having been slowly, and time-wastingly groomed to either work in a shop or in a factory, a common functionary, obliged to 'fit in' and fade out.

That is the way it was. Time rolls on and some threads in life re-connect given enough time.

I mustn't grumble, I had ended up with quite an interesting job, and not in a shop or a factory.

It was weird handing in my notice at work. Having been employed by Co-operative Funeralcare for over twenty years, and like most of the people I worked with, partially institutionalised into a busy regional depot of the Co-operative 'family' as they like to call it.

I was therefore not really focussed on the insecurities and potential challenges of dramatic life-changes suddenly happening.

I went into the main office area at a quiet, and suitably discreet time and slipped my letter of resignation under the regional manager's door. No fuss, no farewells, no sentimental 'keep-in-touch' bullshit.

I was having none of it.

That would have been fake.

One big thing I learned whilst being a funeral director in a big city was that at the end of it all, no one gives a damn save for a few tears from decent people and beneficiaries. We live, we piss, we shit, we eat, we die, one of billions of players each acting their part on the stage of life... really, and in all honesty, a relatively painless life, and a few good friends, and enough to stop us suffering are all we need. Many aspire for more, most are disappointed, if they even realise it!... we need to always remember when desiring to live the dream, that nightmares are dreams too.

Don't be dismayed at my negativity there, it's uncharacteristic of me but I'm sure you are aware of the need for stoic realism.

The Co-operative was one of the reasons, over time the Institution had, in my experience become progressively more negative and careless in delivering service to the community.

Funeral prices were going up too quickly, resources were getting increasingly inferior, and senior management were simply out of touch with what was going on. They were managing by omission and default. Negativity and insensitivity manifested itself increasingly over time to such an extent that I was actually glad to be leaving when I did. I still feel sorry for the decent people who have no choice but to remain in the grind of it all.

… and I left not a moment too soon as it happened.

Sure, it was a step into the unknown as I was effectively volunteering to be an unemployed carer for my mother who needed looking after in her own house, and putting her into an old peoples home as is the social norm in Britain would be more of a drain to family income than me giving up work.

Realistically, the cost ratio made a residential care home twice as expensive as me not working at all. At least I had my hobbies, primarily whisky, whisky reviews and assorted spirity-stuff.

Now there was something else I had more of... precious, precious **time**.

Time to do somethings', nothings', more, less, whatevers!

Sometimes we need the grace to resign ourselves to the turbulence of living, that unforeseen changes bring into our lives, rather than be resigned to a foreseen same-ness of a lesser life, which is too easy to accommodate.

Sometimes we need to admit that the fates decide our life's circumstances, not us.

We can only do our best to influence that which we have no choice but to accept.

It's often a subtle thing where hindsight either verifies or vilifies our actions taken.

As soon as I arrived on the island, I unloaded what was left of my whisky collection into my mum's house and stacked up a cupboard in the spare room with hundreds of bottles of whisky.

The collection at this point was exceeding two thousand bottles, and with careful planning and a few good and trustworthy friends I managed to split the whisky collection up into four stashes of five hundred bottles in each location. This made sense from a safety point of view as fewer bottles in a single stash are less bottles to steal, also house insurance issues are another factor, after all, stating for a fire and contents claim with one's insurer that there were actually two thousand liquor bottles 'going off' in the house fire might not get a lot of sympathy from those processing the claim for a pay out.

I'm sure there will be a clause somewhere...

In a courageous act of self-control I ensured there were never any more than fifty bottles of single malt open at any one time.

Obviously I needed a new location to record my ongoing whisky reviews, and it was important not to simply recreate the little studio that I had set up in my Glasgow home. I needed a different studio for my new and different location, something more traditional and old-worldly preferably!

The first recording called whisky review 178 which was a rather tasty ten year old Springbank was a disaster as the first recording location was all wrong and it simply did not work. The set-up with me in my mother's house reclining in a comfy seat under a large oak mantelpiece in front of a roaring fire sort of Scottish baronial style was impressive enough, but just not 'me'.

It was not *right*!

I abandoned the first recording for a few days and attended to the over-growing garden instead.

It was whilst I was in the garden shed which was part of an eighteenth century stone bothy, that I tripped over a digging fork and smacked my face painfully as the handle sprang up!

I stopped and considered the situation further as it had suddenly occurred to me that what I was currently standing in, and trying to un-clutter forks, rakes, spades and a rusty lawn mower was in fact similar in style and appearance to an old Inn that I once visited in the highlands of Scotland. The bare white-washed stones were basic and functional, far from cosmetic and totally in keeping with some rustic, old bothy-bar in the middle of nowhere, somewhere Scottish and remote.

I de-cluttered the gardening stuff outside against a wall and into an organised heap which I covered temporarily with a tarpaulin to keep the rain off, then set to clearing out the rubbish and accumulated junk from the remaining small stone room.

Once cleared, I could see the growing potential for a good location.

The fireplace was still open in the corner adding a characterful triangular shaped aperture. and having had a look up the chimney, I could see it was clear of blockages and clearly fit for use, a bothy without a fireplace for warmth and cheer is simply no use.

A heavy wood work bench remained in position across one of the outside windows, and on clearing it of all the dust, cobwebs and debris, it was obviously too sturdy to knock down easily, so I left it in place. A quick check with a measuring tape showed that, if needed, a few empty ex-bourbon barrels could be safely and securely stacked along the bench, which would successfully reproduce an authentic dunnage warehouse feel to the place, further adding to the ambience and authenticity of the location. Soon the space was empty, cleaned, assessed and some rustic furnishings placed around the room to give that basic feel of utility and purpose.

I did not have to wait long for the rain to arrive, sluggish and lazy as it sprinkled down from the sky, as slow and warm as the late summer day in which it fell.

I could hear the pitter patter of rain on the roof slates above my head, but none came through the roof and into the bothy reassuring me that it was still a water tight space. All good, and time for a well earned cup of tea.

There now follows an interlude to my story.

Let me give you some traditional advice about British tea from a British person.

Loose, good quality tea leaves are added to a pre-warmed teapot using an ornate teaspoon, preferably, to a glazed ceramic teapot of aesthetic character and in an appropriate ambient environment which is fine if you want to go a bit over the top, but in the real world grab a cheap but substantial mug which will hold roughly half a pint of hot liquid and drop a teabag into the mug. Do not place the teabag in, throw it in!

Allow the kettle to boil completely till the automatic switch turns off, then allow about ten seconds for the boiling sound to stop coming from the kettle. Add the non-boiling, but still very hot water into the mug ensuring the teabag gets agitated by the added hot water. Leave the bag to 'stew' for about five minutes staring repeatedly at the growing brown colour of the contents, then add spoons of sugar if required, or if not, just add a small drop of about five to eight millilitres of semi-skimmed milk, and press the teabag against the inside of the mug with the back of your teaspoon. Thereafter, remove the used teabag and add it to your compost heap, or flick it into a convenient bin with some aggression.

Do not attempt to stir the mug again otherwise you might dissolve too much of the added sugar.

Place down the teaspoon in an inconvenient place and lift the hot mug of tea to your lips, sip, taste then go "aaaaaah" thereafter concluding with the honoured time-traditional phrase "Can't beat a good cuppa!"

On completion of the tea, abandon your empty mug where you are most likely to forget where you put it, this too is traditional.

There is a reason I mention this. Smell and taste is influenced by routine and protocols. The *ceremony* and routine employed in making a decent cuppa tea is very similar to that used in preparing for pouring a wee dram of scotch into a suitable glass, and thereafter enjoying it slowly and with gravitas. Location is important.

Whisky, like tea needs a suitable location for ambient focus on the complete event for virtue of the profound satisfaction of the experience. My Manx bothy is this location.

Old, solid, rustic, a bit draughty, elemental, and a fireplace, flickering flames, bookcase, shadows, silence. Perfect.

NO television, bright lights, media, sports conversations.

None of that, more like a philosophers cavern, imbued with the spirit of fire and water.

A place of earth and metal in a flux of air and ether.

This would be my Avalon, my Sherwood, my Valhalla... my whisky muse.

I rolled out a barrel from my garage, kept there as a spare for the staves, and leveraged it into the newly cleared bothy, up-ending it so as to provide a suitable table of sorts, and on discovering a brass triskelion wall mounting, I attached that to the wall behind me so as to add provenance to the location.

A triskelion is a three sided sun-symbol popular with the celts and vikings way back in the days of old. It is the national symbol of the Isle of Man where the three sides take the form of human legs with spurs. All very occult really.

Finally, with a barrel, a bookcase and a wall-mounting in place, I needed one more feature to confirm that the bothy was a YouTube video vlog studio, and this came in the form of a paint swatch obtained free from the local hardware store. Colours selected matched perfectly with what one might consider 'whisky colours', mainly browns, amber and yellow. I wrote on it in permanent marker 'ralfy.com' which seemed appropriate as an identity and copyright symbol.

I recorded my first video, the sound was awful!

With the stone walls and lack of furniture, the sound was bouncing all over the place distorting the recording quality badly... and the solution? ... to hang bed sheets (clean ones) from the roof beams in order to break up the distortion. It was a home-spun solution which worked a treat.

I was now ready to record my first whisky review in the Manx bothy!

Springbank ten year old single malt, there could be no better choice.

I forgot the malt-mention at the start in all the excitement.

My new, warmer fleece jacket made me look like a stuffed toy teddy bear, which was not a good look, and was soon changed for something better!

I gave the malt eighty six out of one hundred as a malt-mark.

That seemed reasonable and realistic, and it was an honest opinion, after all, I'm not an expert, and I never want to be considered one.

I was very comfortable in the bothy for the first recording and there has been many a summers night since then, where I have sat there in the calm of a gentle breeze whispering around the walls, the fire flickering, all restfully restless and glowing cosy, and I have enjoyed many fine quality malt-moments all by myself and happily shared with the silence.

Don't get me wrong, I do enjoy company and a good malt-chat, however the complex layers and versions of both flavours and sensations respond well to contemplation over time, uninterrupted by chitter-chatter about other stuff, which is always the formality of company however positive and amicable.

One of the actual problems of drinking good whiskies with company is the increased risk of suggestibility, where someone, or several people, will contribute comment on form, flavours and quality of liquor which will directly or indirectly influence how we view it.

What needs to be considered here is the subliminal need by a commenter to have their view accepted by the present company thus endorsing their palate and opinion. This will of course be influenced by the sensitivity of their nose, their experience with liquors, their preferences to accent certain flavours they spot, and which make them happy, and also to blind-side any flavours they are not so keen on. This in turn causes auto-suggestibility that this person has their personal and valid assessment, and therefore what they are experiencing is what we should be experiencing too.

Except, we are all a little bit different, as are our whisky experiences.

Brand ambassadors do this all the time as they are sales-people selling product, which is their job.

"Look at this fabulous, rich, dark colour", they say as they hold a glass up, literally elevating it physically higher in the presence of the audience to 'lift' its status.

Then the glass gets swirled dramatically, shaken, held in an impractical way then swept up to the commenters nose, first one nostril, then past the the other nostril, then back to the first nostril and all theatrically done for maximum preparatory drama, "Aaaahhhh". gasps the ambassador "Such a rich, full, complex and substantial aroma with such bouquets, evocative, quality, nostalgic ethereal. *Dark,* profound, impactful"... and my favourite descriptor, *satisfying!*

This is all about presentative theatre and up-selling by suggestion, and to make it worse, as we consume more alcohol we get more suggestible.

A sip is taken by the brand ambassador, framed with a look of sober contemplation and academic earnestness, then the pause, there's always a pause, sometimes waaaaay too long, a 'magic moment' is now manufactured and in preparing the audience for the punch-line, the sip stops, liquor swallowed, then more superlatives such as "So clean", "Smooooth", "Fresh", "Fruity", "Peaty", etc.

The free hand not actually holding the glass is waved about for drama.

A bit of name-dropping of 'status' people like blenders, famous customers and personalities within the Industry may be uttered quickly, that most folk attending may not know anyway, but are sprinkled around the conversation like pixie dust.

"Isn't that just simply the *best* whisky you've ever tasted?", is the conclusion of the confident host.

It's very entertaining when one first experiences the situation but after a few such happenings, it gets a bit boring, repetitive and predictable.

All good brand ambassadors should in fact avoid blunt, suggestibility monologue. Instead, asking of the audience what they find they are experiencing, followed by the time-line of the experiences, so for example, "How do you find the arrival on your tongue?", "Do you notice any prominent flavour notes in the development?"

"How long and intense is the finish on your palate?".

By asking light and open questions to an audience, rather than imposing suggestibility-script onto the room creates a better rapport, with the event becoming a little more interactive and communicable. This in turn is more interesting and less boring for the audience.

There are risks of course that one of the audience may be a bit too 'interactive' or even be a plonker, however, with experience an ambassador will pick up the warning signs early on and hopefully close-down the threat of an audience member dictating the tone of the tasting.

I understand the constraint placed on brand ambassador sales-people. They have to stick to a script much of the time, and even then be circumspect on what they say, and the comments they make, so it is understandable that they stick to smells and flavour expletives. One problem they face is that over the course of a tast-ing the audience are experiencing more and more liquor which will create it own 'verbalising' and confidence of opinion which may manifest in awkward questions to the presenter, or worse, unflatter-ing comments about experiences with the products the ambassador is representing.

In the old days the allure of good value ticket prices and eti-quette would be enough to assure behaviour moderation within an audience, but not so much now.

A lot has changed, and it is frequently the occasion that one or more audience members will know more about a distillery than the presenter acting as the distilleries ambassador.

This, they will possibly make known to everyone.

Traditional advertising for whisky, especially recently, is per-ceived by many to be lack-lustre, unimaginative and boring. One reason for this is the large amount of red-tape and regulation sur-rounding what can, and cannot feature in an alcohol advert. To-bacco faced this same situation many years ago until it was discov-ered to be too dangerous to health to advertise at all.

Cigarette adverts in particular would often not even mention or show the product but still be effective in selling product.

With whisky there seems to be a bit more 'give' in messaging, with glasses of amber nectar being shown in mood-lit, urbane envi-ronments such as gentlemens clubs, highland glens and distillery warehouses, with "long years", "rich history" and "established since"... sprinkled round the fringes of the ad.

That's the beauty of the internet, online commentators *SHOULD NOT* be brand ambassadors sitting in the cheap seats of marketing budgets waiting for malt-crumbs and compliments.

The internet is there to provide the antithesis of the traditional marketing routines.

The internet in blogs and vlogs is there to offer a different take on whisky and other spirits by offering personality, opinion, views, commentary, rants, criticism, likes, dislikes, problems, faults and flaws, and all done in good faith and without nastiness or specific trolling.

Mercifully, compared to other 'categories' of internet focus, the whisky scene is remarkably civilised and civil, with most contributors decent and worthy human beings brought together by appreciation and concord of the malt-moment, shared by default, and understood by everyone who drinks. Whilst online fashion, sport, politics and entertainment commentaries are rife with vicious trolling and trash-talk, the whisky scene online remains a relatively tranquil back-water of decency and polite comment, feedback and patience with a ready willingness by experienced maltsters to offer advice and support with recommendations to any enquiries from inexperienced novices. Whisky along with other quality spirits made for sipping, not swigging, appears to build bridges in collective human goodwill.

So far the Scotch Whisky Industry has been generally lucky in the calibre and enthusiasm of online content, which often exceeds the reach and influence of traditional marketing by a significant margin and will continue to do so over the next few years.

There exists online, a broad-minded inclusiveness by the global whisky community towards an industry which lazily tub-thumps about the 'exclusivity' of its product, all twenty six million barrels of 'exclusivness'. (as at 2019). Now is the time to promote 'inclusive', not 'exclusive'.

All the Industry needs to do now is develop a better maturity, and appreciation for these, often tolerated anoraks, not just the commentators, but also the social media users who text, tweet, Facebook and Snapchat ongoing positivity and enthusiasm for products which the Industry is increasingly charging more and more money for.

Is it greed?

Yes it is a bit.

Some Distilleries are a lot less greedy than others. All over-endowed marketing professionals tend to be greedy as this translates into financial bonuses, and many senior managers within the Industry really need to take regular reality-checks to recalibrate market tolerances towards inflating bottle prices. Don't get me wrong, there are many good people, but being 'real life', there are also bampot decision makers too... just the way it goes!

Apart from the occasional rant and blooper in my vlogs, I am happy in what I continue to create in terms of context and content.

The Manx Bothy has been the home for nine years now of weekly recordings of vlogs with each vlog often featuring a new bottle of age-stated quality spirit, usually Scotch malt whisky, but also rum, bourbon and rye spirits occasionally to add variety. It's hard, but I cope!

Some spirits are re-reviewed periodically due to possible changes over the years in smell and taste, and additional information, views, experiences and opinion are provided in the 'extras' vlogs where I recognise the value to many drinkers of the experiences beyond basic smell and taste which add to the enjoyment of liquor.

It's the ethanol you see! It is unique in the chemical world in chemo-physically bonding the wide-ranging soup of flavonoids onto ethanol molecules in such a way that these flavourants will hold their integrity for hundreds, if not thousands of years, before fading. Nothing is more complex on the palate than cask-flavoured and matured spirits, especially delicate spirits like malted barley whisky.

My 'personal' time is from ten at night to three in the morning, this is when my dear old mother who has dementia, is reliably asleep. At this point I can properly rest, as I am no longer on mother-watch wondering every minute of the day whether she is having a fall, making a mess, or trying to electrocute herself by pulling wires out of plugs, the sort of thing many dementia'd people do.

I care for her willingly, and as a bonus for my care and consideration she only stole my whisky once.

It was seven o'clock in the morning and I was still half asleep and not quite ready for what was happening downstairs in the kitchen.

I had left a bottle of Bladnoch sitting by the kettle where I had made another cup of tea before heading off to bed the previous night.

The old darling, by now in her eighties, had taken a shine to the bottle and uncharacteristically opened it and started drinking the contents, fortunately there was not that much left, but still enough to get her well and truly 'pished'. She had, in anticipation of the pending intoxication, walked through to the front room and picked up a large fluffy cushion which she hugged tightly to her chest keeping it firmly in place as she finally stumbled and fell flat on her face in the hallway.

The cushion worked a treat.

Undamaged, I carried her up stairs and put her back into her little bed where she gurgled, smiled a lot and mumbled sweet nothings about anything, whilst I spoon fed her water to alleviate the forthcoming hangover.

I mentioned the situation to the visiting district nurse the following week as she did her rounds.

The nurse laughed, most oldies she attended to simply resorted to vodka rather than malts!

Thereafter, I ensured all bottles were secured against any further 'misunderstandings'.

My mother's most favourite tipple ended up being hot milk and Crabbies ginger wine, she loved the stuff and slept well on it. She needed no prescription medication from the doctor and therefore took none. This, I'm sure, helped her to live longer and better thanks to the care my brother Clive and I provided.

To be honest, at this moment in time I was drinking more than was good for me, it's a risk after all of being a whisky 'enthusiast', it can become an exotic cover-story for being an up-market, hard-drinker. The situation resolved itself naturally.

I'm out in the Bothy again, it's a fine silent and sublime sum-mer's night, the birds are no longer singing having settled in their nests, and the remains of the day glow as do the embers in the fire-place, rosy, warm and comforting. I make a computer Skype call to Singapore, after all, if one wants to know what is happening in China, one needs to know the right bar to phone in Singapore, and call at the right time to speak to the right person.

I follow up with a call to Argentina, chatting for an hour to a wine grower in the mountains who wants to diversify away from wine to brandy, and wonders if Carmenere grapes will be usable. Finally I call the Caribbean, Barbados, to speak to a shipper who is thinking of opening a rum distillery as a tourist attraction, but wants to get it right and possibly source Scottish copper pot stills. He seems fazed and less sure when I suggest the costs involved and the time-line.

Phone calls are over, global conversations in an ever shrinking World where village gossip is now trans-national, and I return my attention to some unfinished Talisker. Eighteen years old as stated on the bottle label, where the information matters, and it's totally delicious too.

I smell, sip, savour and listen intensely to the silence.

An African philosopher once observed that silence is a good companion, "he listens very well and will never judge our deeds" said the philosopher who was wise and worldly, someone worth quoting more than once!

I reach for some African whisky, tucked away on the shelf, I pour a glass and raising it high, offer a toast to Africa, the silence offers applause for my accord.

I am no longer sober, but I am not yet intoxicated.

Somewhere in between there is a place of deeper meaning, a bliss point, a golden, glowing moment which will not last long, but remains long enough to offer a deeper emotional and instinctive vi-sion by ourselves into our souls and the soul of the universe.

It does not happen every time, it needs a special circumstance within a special place to really happen.

It happens tonight, I bask in the glow, part awake, part sober, part tipsy, part detached, part disconnected from the *now*. I know how to caress this situation, to make it last a bit longer although never long enough. Time swirls around the Bothy, a silent breeze of universal energy, of chi, of ki, of ley, of prana, of infinity, and I release its spell over me with reluctance, as nightfall makes my sleepy unfocussing eyes ever more heavy from the weight of the days concerns.

I stagger from bothy to bed and tumble deep into sublime, dreamless, oblivion aware as I fade from the now, that tomorrow is always, and only ever will be, another today, and life is good to me and I will it to be so.

Briefly, swiftly, somewhere down the glen, and off in the distance, as sleep surges like an incoming tide, I hear the sound of a weaving loom being worked, and somewhere deep in the woodland between the bothy and the Irish sea a weaver is weaving,

clickety click,

clickety click,

clickety clock,

clickety clock,

on and on and ever on, with his tweel and threads he weaves to the sound of music and time, looming a rich tapestry of bright and moody colours, line after line after line, of thread upon thread. He weaves reality and illusion, mystery and sunrise, story and legend, folklore and history and I smile to myself as it all fades, knowing as I do that someday we will meet, myself and the little weaver, a bright and sprightly small creature, different to me, but no stranger to the woodlands and this world.

Now all is gone, faded until tomorrow, where by then, most is forgotten from the night before, but what little remains is valued and cherished, enlivened once more in a few days or a few weeks or perhaps a month by the virtue of a dram, and good provenance, found within the Bothy and aligned for another special malt-moment still to be woven into the fabric of my life.

I need to conclude this book now malt-mates.

I'm back across in Scotland, a precious near-faraway place that gives me the needed distraction from island life, which I do enjoy, but need to get away from a few times a year.

Paul, the proprietor of the Bon Accord gives me a ruddy-faced grin along with a brisk hand wave as I shuffle into his cosy bustling bar from off of a rain-strewn, wind-ruffled street, alive as it is with the rumble of motorway traffic heading rapidly north, and rapidly south across the City of Glasgow. I have left the City now, but it will never leave me, and I don't want it to. As the entrance door squeeks slightly as people enter and leave, Paul briefly glances to check-up on the customer, in a second he is concluded and we settle for a catch-up chat.

He insists on buying me a pint of something crisp, hopped and I.P.A'ish which I would be rude to refuse. We chat about people, whisky, Glasgow, and anything interesting, and one by one the regulars including Sandy and Ross nudge into the conversation, as do the lively bar staff who add so much to the atmosphere of my favourite spot in Glasgow for a whisky and an ale together, and as one. The Bon Accord, the first bar I ever went into when I was fifteen to collect my dad to take him home in mother's car for our dinner and then my homework for school... and if you were to ask that young lad called Ralfy why he would be back again in this bar all these years later, I really don't think he would believe you.

I wouldn't!

Keep it malty, whisky lovers.

I finally found my whisky bothy.

I hope that you find yours too.

Regards from Ralfy.

Epilogue

The first thing I need to say in concluding this book all about whisky and the characters I have known over the years relating to whisky is... don't over-indulge.

Respect the varied influence that whisky can have and respect yourselves while you're at it.

It's just the way it is... just sayin'!

So I've just poured another dram and raised a wee goldy to salute the clock, which just keeps clicking and ticking out the time, on and on. I pause to reflect on this, the relentless passage of time, and conclude after a few moments of self-reflection that perhaps I should begin work on my second book, 'Tales of a Whisky Drinker', or something like that.

I will use that as my working title, and will get writing shortly.

Thank you for buying my book,

I appreciate it.

Catch up with me on my YouTube channel "ralfydotcom", where I review quality spirits and talk about spirit related stuff.

I also have a second channel on youtube.com called "fitter philosophy", where I walk and talk some practical, philosophical observations. Don't forget to subscribe and leave a comment!

Ralfy.

August 2019.
The Manx Bothy.